12-50
6-25

"What, indeed, is more delightful than a bowl...full of fresh Roses!... All kinds, in their many ways, adapt themselves to good room treatment. There is a delightful freshness of sweet scent in a room newly decked with many Roses."

FLOWER DECORATION
IN THE HOUSE

BY

GERTRUDE JEKYLL

ANTIQUE COLLECTORS' CLUB

ISBN 0 907462 31 6

First published by Country Life/George Newnes Ltd., 1907.
This edition published for the Antique Collectors' Club by
the Antique Collectors' Club Ltd. 1982, with 8 colour
illustrations added.

British Library CIP Data
Jekyll, Gertrude
    Flower decoration in the house.
    1. Flower arrangement
    I. Title
    745.92   SB449

Printed in England by Baron Publishing, Woodbridge, Suffolk

CONTENTS

PAGE

CHAPTER   I. OUTDOOR FLOWERS AND FOLIAGE
NOVEMBER TO FEBRUARY .   9

CHAPTER   II. MARCH   31

CHAPTER III. APRIL AND MAY   37

CHAPTER IV. JUNE   54

CHAPTER   V. JULY   71

CHAPTER VI. AUGUST   81

CHAPTER VII. SEPTEMBER AND OCTOBER .   .   .   87

CHAPTER VIII. ROOM AND CONSERVATORY DECORA-
TION   103

CHAPTER IX. VASES AND HOLDERS FOR POT PLANTS   112

CHAPTER   X. DINNER-TABLES   133

CHAPTER XI. WILD FLOWERS IN THE HOUSE .   150

CHAPTER XII. THE RESERVE GARDEN .   .   .   160

INDEX   166

PREFACE

IN offering some suggestions on the use of flowers in house decorations, the writer is aware how well the matter is already understood in many households. Indeed, flower decoration in rooms is the branch of gardening—for it is a branch of gardening—that of all others has made the most rapid and effective progress.

Of late years much has been done and written to help the growth and general comprehension of the better ways of gardening; those ways that demand not only the cultural ability that can produce the material, but the cultivated taste that can use good plants and flowers to the very best advantage.

In houses of small or average calibre the flowers are generally arranged by the mistress of the house or her daughter. In large houses it is commonly done by the gardener, who also brings in the best of his pot plants, arranges them and attends to the watering. He also provides the plants and flowers for the dinner table, dressing it also with cut flowers and foliage.

Sometimes one of the indoor servants has a great love of flowers and delights in arranging them. Such a one soon acquires much skill, and, with a little out-side help may develop real taste; a quality that is always growing. Just a hint or two about simple schemes of colour and grace of line is often enough to sow the good seed in a receptive mind. Then the happiness of handling the flowers and inventing new and beautiful combinations will both bring its own reward to the operator and produce the good decoration ; thus fulfilling the best purpose of the flower's existence.

The main object of this book is to offer useful suggestions to those who have not had much practice, while it may at the same time remind the more advanced of a few details that have been overlooked. It is assumed that one important part of the subject, that of the hardy flowers that will be available, will be most helpfully dealt with month by month, so that it will not only be a useful form of reference, saying what material is to be had, and in many cases how it may be simply treated ; but may also be a guide to the preparation of that part of the reserve garden in which flowers may be cut to any extent without robbing the more important and well-dressed portions of the pleasure grounds.

G. J.

FLOWER DECORATION IN
THE HOUSE

CHAPTER I

OUTDOOR FLOWERS AND FOLIAGE
NOVEMBER TO FEBRUARY

EVEN in the depth of winter, when flowers are least plentiful, good room decoration may be done with but very few, or indeed with foliage only.

In an average garden that is not quite new, there is always something to be found. A country house is hardly ever without its masses of shrubbery. More than once it has happened that the mistress of such a house bewailed herself to the writer, that there was nothing pickable in the garden ; whereas the old shrubberies were simply unworked mines of endless wealth.

In the latest case, in a comparatively small place, it was easy to show her how much there was only waiting to be used. First there was an old, overgrown Aucuba in a shady place among tall shrubs. Its rather pale green leaves were large and wide, and its branches were flung abroad in a way that would evidently suit a large jar of Italian majolica, that my hostess wished to fill with something worthy.

Many people say they do not like Aucubas. I must

9

confess to a time, now a good many years ago, when I said the same. Searching for the reason, it may be found in the general use or misuse of them in the little tight mixed shrubberies of suburban villas. The Aucuba is a long-suffering thing, and in these ugly little gardens—alas that they should be ugly, for they need not be—it bravely holds its own, and often remains as the liveliest survivor of the cramped tangle of shrubs that are so cruelly packed together. In the same way in seaside places on the south coast, the mind becomes wearied with the forced and unwelcome satiety produced by the endless reiteration of green or golden Euonymus.

Yet both are capital shrubs ; only wanting to be rightly used. On a shady bank of poor sandy soil, even under Scotch Firs, I have seen beautiful bushes of Aucuba ; their bright green leaves glistening with abundant health and vigour, and among them some plants loaded with scarlet berries. In winter the berries are mostly green, and scarcely less handsome, though naturally not so showy. It is a bush that looks best in a fair mass together ; in some quiet place of twilight half-shade, in company with bold tufts of hardy ferns and a restricted number of flowering plants, such as Solomon's Seal and white Columbine ; a kind of place the furthest possible in sentiment from the fussy unrest of the roadside shrubbery, enduring as well as it may the endless showerings of chimney-blacks and smotherings of road-dust.

The most vigorous in growth of the garden varieties of Aucuba is the one with yellow-spotted leaves. A

AUCUBA BRANCHES IN A MAJOLICA JAR.

ARUMS WITH BROAD-LEAVED LAUREL IN MAJOLICA.

branch or two of this in any large jar, preferably one of the blue and white Oriental porcelain, is a fine winter ornament.

All this was pointed out to my hostess, and it was pleasant to see her growing interest as she became aware of the value of the material that could be biought into use. "We will have some side boughs of the Aucuba," I said, "and I see some straight shoots of a Laurel beyond it, that will do to go with those Arum flowers we saw in the greenhouse." It was the broad-leaved Laurel; the one known as "round-leaved" in nurseries. The pieces chosen were some with unusually large leaves of a bright pale-green colour. They looked as if they had grown quickly under some unusual stimulus, such as a sudden spell of heat and moisture during the past summer, and they had escaped damage from winter cold from their sheltered place near the middle of the bush, so that in general effect they were Laurel branches with leaves unusually large, and yet refined by being of softer texture; branches that made one think rather of a Greek mountain side than of a neglected English shrubbery.

A little further was a batch of Berberis; some of it finely coloured. It was easy to choose some straggling pieces nearly three feet long, with good tops of different outward inclination; some nearly upright, and others bending to right and left; and a good branching piece for the middle. Then, greatest prize of all, against a garden shed, was an old bush of the yellow-bloomed winter Jasmine (*Jasminum nudiflorum*) in full flower. Some large and long branches with their pendulous front sprays were soon cut, to be arranged with the Berberis.

By now we were fully loaded, but we had to stop again to examine an old tree of golden Holly. A search among the lower branches produced what was hoped for—some small twigs whose leaves were pale yellow all over :—"These will be charming in one of your silver bowls with just a few white flowers, Christmas Roses or small white Hyacinths."

It may safely be said that a raid in any old shrubbery will produce—not necessarily exactly this—but enough material of like utility, such as, eked out with a very few flowers, will suffice for satisfactory room decoration.

The hardy outdoor flowers of the winter months are of course very few, but the first fortnight of November is rich in the ample supply of bloom given by the true hardy Chrysanthemums. It is only on very rare occasions, such as the unusual occurrence of three nights of severe frost early in October 1905 that the flower buds are so much crippled that the bloom is spoilt. It may safely be said that in nine Novembers out of ten these capital flowers may be depended on. Among the most useful kinds are "Cottage Pink"; "Sœur Mélanie," warm white; "Julie Lagravère," dark red; and "Soleil d'or," orange. The two last are of large pompon size. After slight frosts the foliage of "Cottage Pink" turns to a fine crimson colour, harmonising well with the crimson centre of the not over-blown flower.

HARDY NOVEMBER CHRYSANTHEMUM "COTTAGE PINK."

BERRIES OF IRIS FOETIDISSIMA IN A PEWTER TANKARD.

CHRISTMAS ROSES, PERNETTYA BERRIES AND LAURUSTINUS, WITH HART'S TONGUE FERN.

Another material for room decoration to be looked out for early in November is the long-stalked pods of berries of *Iris fœtidissima*. It is a native plant whose ornamental qualities are often overlooked, but for its vigorous dark green glossy foliage alone it deserves a place in every garden, preferably in half shade, on the cool side of some wall or building. The flowers, that come in summer, are small, dull of colour and of no ornamental value, but the handsome berries more than make up for the poverty of the bloom.

Among the kinds of foliage that are good to use in winter, that of *Cineraria maritima* should not be forgotten. It is still in good order in the earlier winter months, though later it looks a little unhappy.

The second half of November brings the large early Christmas Rose (*Helleborus altifolius*), the first of the true winter flowers. The later forms of the same plant bloom through December and January and into February. If space can be allowed in a cold greenhouse or any such place it is well to have some strong clumps in tubs for cutting. The bloom comes large and pure and long-stemmed, and in better order all round than from the open ground.

Another true winter flower that is now in general cultivation is the Algerian *Iris stylosa*, otherwise *Iris unguicularis*. Like the Christmas Rose it opens its first blooms in November, but its season is still longer, for it goes on until April. Anywhere in the latitude of London, and still better in the warmer climate of the south coast, this delightful flower and its varieties may be grown ; and in all open weather, on well-established

Gertrude Jekyll's lively imagination meant she saw winter gardens as "unworked mines of endless wealth... Even in the depth of winter, when flowers are least plentiful, good room decoration may be done with but very few, or indeed with foliage only... a raid in any old shrubbery will produce... enough material... such as, eked out with a very few flowers, will suffice for satisfactory room decoration." Christmas Roses, Holly and sprayed foliage and flowers.

clumps, the charming light blue-purple, sweet-scented flowers will be open. Near London it is thankful for the protection of a wall; and if it is the wall of a greenhouse, or any heated structure, so much the better. The only precaution it needs is to see that it is not too kindly treated as to soil, for, if this is too rich, the plant will make great tufts of leaves a yard long, and give no flowers, or but very few. Its own leaves are, in any case, rather too long to arrange with it when cut, but there is a capital little plant, with sword-shaped leaves of somewhat the same character, that does admirably with it as well as with other smallish winter flowers, such as Freesia, Roman Hyacinth and forced Lily of the Valley. This is *Ophiopogon spicatum*, shown with the Iris in the illustration. It is a hardy plant easily grown ; the foliage is at its best in winter. The flower, which comes later, is of no importance. The leaves grow in convenient sheaves, and the way is to lift a whole tuft, wash out the earth, and cut away the roots, leaving the stock with the leaves just as they grow.

The leaves of Christmas Roses are too precious to be cut, for the plant needs them all ; indeed no Hellebore leaves should be cut off, at least not until they are quite brown and dry right down the stalk ; but it is a good plan to have a reserve of the wild Hellebore (*H. fœtidus*) grown for the purpose of providing leaves. Christmas Roses are also handsome with leaves of some of the Megaseas, the best of these being those of the *cordifolia* section. *M. cordifolia major* has very fine leaves, waved at the edge, and with a crumpled

IRIS STYLOSA.

CHRISTMAS ROSE, LAURUSTINUS AND FOLIAGE OF MEGASEA IN A MUNSTEAD GLASS.

corrugation of surface that throws them into bold forms of light and shade. These suit the Hellebore flowers well, although they are so entirely unlike their own foliage.

Laurustinus, in our milder districts, is in bloom more or less throughout the winter ; a few sprays are shown with the Hellebore and Megasea leaves in the glass bowl. For the best part of our climate there is the still better *Laurustinus lucidus,* with larger, whiter flowers in looser clusters, and handsome leaves, fresh, bright and highly polished, a noble shrub of the most refined beauty both indoors and out.

The yellow Jasmine (*Jasminum nudiflorum*) is well known. Bloom can be cut from it throughout the winter in all open weather, but frost spoils the expanded flowers. It is therefore advisable to have covers of some material like Willesden scrim, and some arrangement whereby these can be easily hooked up or removed, according to the weather. It is usual to grow it against a wall or fence, so that this should not be a difficult matter.

For ordinary garden decoration it should be remembered that there is also another use for this capital winter-blooming shrub. Its habit may be described as straggling-pendulous ; fitting it for use among stiffer bushes, or for tumbling about in rocky places. In many pleasure-grounds, where the land is steeply graded, or especially in half-wild places, where rising banks occur or ascending broken ground, such a planting as common white Thorn, kept in bush form, with the yellow Jasmine trained through and over, will show the rambling plant to great advantage ; and the partial protection will save much of the bloom from frost.

Arbutus furnishes many a delightful branch and twig of flower and even fruit in the winter months, but it is happiest in the south.

Of all the lovely forms of branch and leaf, the one that may be said to be of supremest beauty—that of the Sweet Bay—may be enjoyed in winter. For then the whole bush, or tree as it is in the south, is at its best and glossiest. To any one who has a keen delight in the beauty of form, that of a twig of Bay is little less than amazing. The stem is slender but strong, the leaves are beautifully set on ; the leaf itself, with its richly waved edge telling of strength, its tough and yet refined texture, its firm pale green midrib—again for strength ; its form, broadly lance-shaped, narrowing to a finely-pointed tip that inclines downward—the whole structure showing the most admirable design for strength and beauty, grace and refinement—is truly a thing to marvel at, and to have and hold with the utmost reverence and thankfulness.

The foliage of Ilex or Evergreen Oak is singularly becoming to many winter flowers. The illustration (p. 26) shows it arranged with a bunch of Scilly White Narcissus in early February. It should be remembered that the Ilex leaves are at their best in winter. By April they become spotted and discoloured, and a few weeks later the young growths will be sprouting.

There are several shrubs with variegated foliage that are of great use in winter decorations. One of the best of these is the gold-variegated Privet, holding

A BRANCH OF BAY.

NARCISSUS SCILLY WHITE WITH FOLIAGE OF ILEX.

its leaves till well after Christmas ; a worthy companion to the winter yellow Jasmine and any white flowers. The variegated Elæagnus is also a capital thing ; the branches and twigs are extremely stiff-wooded, and when they are arranged they form a strong scaffolding for the introduction and support of any flowers that are to go with them. They are also long-enduring in water, and for this reason are admirable companions for long-lived flowers, such as free-sprayed stove Orchids. The gold-variegated Euonymus, both narrow and broad-leaved, is also of much value for winter cutting.

Where there is a warm wall or some building that affords shelter to well-grown specimens of Loquat, a branch or two of its grand foliage is, even alone, a fine winter decoration. *Magnolia grandiflora,* if of mature growth, may also spare some of its glossy leafage.

In January and February there will be the deliciously sweet flowers of the Winter-Sweet (*Chimonanthus fragrans*). To get the best yield of bloom the shrubs should be pruned hard to short spur-like growths. It is not convenient to cut it in sprays, but the little half-transparent yellowish blooms are picked straight off the wood and floated in shallow dishes. They are charming in anything of a flat tazza form.

For flowering in February it is useful to prepare, the November before, a quantity of pots of Crocuses of different sizes ; the smallest to hold only three to five bulbs, in preparation for planting out when blooming time comes, in some rather wide receptacles. Deep

dishes either of china or pewter are as good as any,
or, if the holder admits of having a zinc liner, they can
be planted at once in the liner, which has drainage
holes in the bottom. They are prettiest if they are

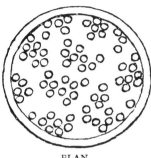

PLAN

planted irregularly, as shown in the diagram. This
can be best done by planting at once in the liner.
When in bloom and brought into the room, they
should be surfaced with the nicest moss that can be
obtained, the moss being brought over the edge of the
liner and half-way over the edge of the dish. When
the outer receptacle is of such a size and shape that a

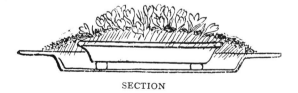

SECTION

round garden seed-pan can be used inside, it is all the
better, as it is rather more suitable for planting in than
zinc. In any case it ought to stand clear of the outer

dish at the bottom, which is easily managed by letting
it stand on a few sections of cork or slips of wood.
In this way the bulbs would not be water-logged, and
by tipping the dish daily the surplus water can be
poured off. Crocuses so treated are surprisingly
bright and cheerful in a sunny window in the later
days of winter. Others of the early bulbs whose
normal blooming time is March, such as the charming
little Scillas and Chionodoxas, can also be had
in flower a month earlier by potting and gentle
forcing.

Hyacinths need hardly be mentioned ; the method
of forcing and use in rooms being so well known.
Tulips, gently forced in the same way, are beautiful in
rooms ; some of the best being the early pinks and
rosy-reds, such as Rose Gris-de-lin, Cottage Maid and
Rosa Mundi.

In large places there will be stove-grown Orchids
throughout the year, including winter. No flowers
last so long when cut ; many kinds remaining in beauty
for several weeks. The more branching kinds are best
set up with large leaves of Aspidistra, or the fronds of
some wide-spreading fern, such as *Pteris tremula*, one
of the best of the house-ferns for indoor decoration.

Where there are roomy receptacles, the cut Orchid
of largely-branching habit may be with advantage
grouped with the whole fern growing in a pot.
The natural disposition of the fronds of growing
ferns is so good that it is difficult to imitate with any
artificial arrangement of them cut ; besides, cut fern-
fronds do not live long in water, even if they have had

the preparatory overhead soaking that nearly all of them require.

Orchids are not so often used as room-plants as they might well be. The special ways of watering and needs of temperature may make many of them unsuitable, but probably the chief reason why they are so seldom seen in rooms is that their pots or baskets are of so broad a shape that they are awkward things to fit into the usual receptacles. This, however, is only a matter of shirking the trouble of providing holders of suitable form. This subject is dealt with separately in a further part of the book.

CHAPTER II

MARCH

MARCH, from the point of view of its flowers, is a sort of intermediate month, standing out by itself. Our supplies of cut flowers of any size are from the greenhouse, Arums for instance.

Among the lesser pleasures of life is one that occurs occasionally—rather often, in fact, to people who are on the look-out—namely, the making use, and sometimes very good use indeed, of what are commonly looked upon as waste products.

One of the duties of the time of year in the garden is to look out for and remove the suckers of grafted Rhododendrons. The stock is the common *R. ponticum*, which has a narrow, dark green, polished leaf, quite distinct from that of the scion. Some of these will be tall, straight shoots with handsome foliage ; the very thing to arrange with long-stemmed Arums. With occasional changes of the water and fresh flowers, the Rhododendron branches can be used for a month or more, with the alternative of the broad-leaved Laurel, already mentioned.

Towards the end of the month, in many country places, there is an abundance of the wild Arum, which can be well used with the Arum flowers of the greenhouse. The largest should be chosen, the whole bunch of leaves being brought up with a steady pull. The white underground stem then breaks off close to the root. To ensure their living well, they should be plunged into deep pails of water, so that the leaves are partly submerged, and so left for some hours; or it may be done overnight in preparation for arranging next day. Wild Arum leaves of a smaller size are also useful for putting with the earlier Daffodils (p. 40).

In March we have, besides the first Daffodils, the Lent Hellebores or Lenten Roses. They are the garden varieties of *Helleborus atrorubens, H. colchicus, H. olympicus,* and *H. orientalis.* They are purplish-red and greenish-white for the most part, but the many garden hybrids show much diversity of colouring and spotting. Their colouring is never bright, but to an observer of colour, in the artist's sense of the word, it s pleasing and interesting.

They require the same preparation as that just described for wild Arum leaves, with the addition that the cut ends of the stalks should be slit up about two inches, the better to imbibe the water. They are best arranged with stiff branches of Berberis; among these it is easy to arrange the flowers so as to counteract their natural inclination to hang their heads. The reddest flower among the red kinds is never more than a low-toned purple; but the same tones, and some brighter, may be found among the Berberis leaves, and the two together may be made into a whole series of excellent colour harmonies, the white varieties serving to brighten up the bouquet. These

ARUMS WITH FOLIAGE OF WILD ARUM.

MAGNOLIAS OF MARCH AND APRIL.

are also charming alone with some of the brightest green Berberis leaves that can be found.

The end of March brings the bloom of the deciduous *Magnolia conspicua;* pure white cups faintly scented like the larger *Magnolia grandiflora* of the later summer. It is only safe against a wall, and even there should be carefully watched, so that in the event of frost or heavy rain occurring when the flowers are at their best they may receive some protection. Some blooms of this fine Magnolia usually remain till the smaller *M. stellata* is in flower in the earlier weeks of April.

Anemone fulgens will now be in bloom. It the soil is not calcareous, it will be grateful for some chalky addition, such as old lime rubbish. The brilliant scarlet blossom lasts long in water. It is pretty arranged with some flowering sprays of Laurustinus, a few of which may be found in some sheltered corner.

The second half of March brings the strongest bloom of Violets. Even a very few Violets will scent a whole room. They are most manageable if they are arranged in the hand with all the ends of the stalks even, so that the heads are uneven ; a few leaves should be picked and put among them. A bunch of Violets is at its least beautiful in the form usually seen in shops, with the flowers all brought to one level and ringed with a stiff frill of leaves. Then when a few bunches are brought indoors, the ties should be relaxed. The old-fashioned heavy cut finger-glasses, with a glass tumbler stood inside, are capital things for holding them.

It is worth cutting a few branches of the red-leaved Plum, *Prunus Pissardi*, when in young bud. If they are placed in water in a warm greenhouse, they soon open prettily, and are ready for use in the house. Peach prunings can be bloomed in the same way some weeks earlier.

CHAPTER III

APRIL AND MAY

THESE months hang together in the garden and therefore in its products for house decoration.

Fresh-picked Wallflowers are delightfully sweet in rooms. Hardly any flower is more richly brilliant under artificial light than the so-called blood-red colourings. The purples are beautiful arranged with white Tulips. The purples and browns mingle very pleasantly in the sunlight of the spring garden, though this combination indoors is rather too heavy.

Care should be taken to strip off most of the leaves of cut Wallflowers that will be under water, as they quickly decay, and the water should be often changed, for it soon becomes offensive. This is the case with Stocks also and with flowers of the *Cruciferæ* in general. They belong to the same tribe as cabbages, and most people know only too well the bad smell of decaying cabbage leaves.

The most beautiful flowering shrub of April is the neat and pretty *Magnolia stellata*. A well-established plant is about six feet high and through, and bears its milk-white bloom in the greatest profusion. It grows so freely that whole branches can be cut, each branch having many flowers. These alone, or with some

Of acquiring skill and delight in arranging flowers, Gertrude Jekyll wrote: "Just a hint or two about simple schemes of colour and grace of line is often enough to sow the good seed in a receptive mind. Then the happiness of handling the flowers and inventing new and beautiful combinations will both bring its own reward. . . and produce the good decoration."

sprays of Pyrus Japonica, are charming in rooms, and look especially well in silver bowls.

Daffodils are in profusion in the earlier weeks of April, and towards the middle of the month *Berberis Aquifolium* is in bloom. In this state it arranges well with the largest daffodils ; the great yellow Emperor, the large *bicolor* Empress, Sir Watkin, and the bolder of the flat-crowned kinds. Any large bowl, with a capacious jar standing up in it, does well with such an arrangement. I have done them so with fine effect in one of the great silver punch-bowls with the boldly scalloped edges that are known as Menteths.

It should be remembered that to do a spring garden justice it ought to be a garden of spring flowers and no others. The usual way of growing the early blooming parts where they are to be followed by those of summer, not only restricts the choice but makes it impossible to grow some of the best of the early plants which are perennials, such as *Dielytra*, *Dicentra*, *Doronicum*, Solomon's Seal, Anemones, *Dentaria*, *Uvularia*, *Mertensia*, *Tiarella*, and others. This is a fact that is very commonly overlooked, and, though it does not exactly bear on the subject of flowers for cutting (as cutting does not go on in gardens that are for the display of flower-beauty) yet it is well to mention it at any opportunity. Flowers for cutting should be grown in the reserve garden in narrow beds set apart for the purpose. Four feet is a convenient width for the beds. Here the April flowers will comprise some of the Daffodils, beginning with the yellow trumpet Tenby and the early *Incomparabilis* Stella.

TRUMPET DAFFODILS WITH WILD ARUM LEAVES.

Then will follow the beautiful Leedsi group, the large Sir Watkin and good store of the bright-cupped Barri conspicuus, also the large trumpets Horsfieldi, Emperor and Empress, with the later Grandee and the useful Campernelle Jonquil. Many other kinds of the good Daffodils may well find a place in the cutting garden, but these will be essential and may be taken as a useful restricted selection, but it must include the Poet's Narcissus and its double variety for May.

Anemones are excellent house flowers, lasting long in water and opening well in a sunny window. *Myosotis dissitiflora* should not be forgotten. Like all the Forget-me-nots, it lasts well when cut, and is always prettier than the deeper-coloured forms of *M. sylvatica*. By the end of April, with the last of the Daffodils whose bloom runs on into May with the Poet's Narcissus, the true Jonquil, the Tazzetta group and, latest of all, N. gracilis, we get to the time of Tulips. But before leaving the Daffodils, it should not be forgotten that a charming mixture in a room is the Poet's Narcissus, either single or double, with Sweet-brier, now in sweetest, tenderest leaf ; a charming association both for scent and sight.

There is one of the Star of Bethlehem family, *Ornithogalum nutans*, that is remarkably beautiful in water, arranged with some dark, polished foliage such as that of Portugal Laurel or Japan Privet. It has a rare satin-like quality. The bloom is white and yet scarcely white, but is like white satin in half shade. It lasts long in water and becomes more starry and pretty as the days of its indoor life go by. I only hesitate to recommend it because it becomes one of the worst weeds that can be introduced into a garden ; and, according to my own experience in more than one place, it cannot be eradicated.

The Tulips, putting aside the small Van Thols which I could never think either beautiful or interesting, may be said to begin, for indoor decoration, with those charming pink kinds already named as good for forcing —namely, Rosa Mundi, Rose Gris-de-lin and Cottage Maid. They are quickly followed by a host of others, of which I have found White Swan to be one of the most useful. Chrysolora is a desirable early yellow. These are all cheap bulbs and should be grown in quantity in the reserve garden for cutting.

Meanwhile great sheets of a good garden form of *Myosotis dissitiflora* have been coming into bloom. It is an early Forget-me-not of charming quality, better than the garden forms of *M. sylvestris,* which are so much used in spring gardening. With this we grow in long drifts some of the paler of the best forms of Bunch Primroses. This capital Forget-me-not also arranges charmingly, both indoors and out, with another contemporary, the double Arabis ; also with Primroses of pale canary colour and yellow Alyssum ; the Alyssum arranged cloudily among the other flowers and standing a little above them—all in a rather flat, wide bowl.

I always think that this, the time of Tulips, is the season of all the year when the actual arranging of flowers affords the greatest pleasure. The rush and heat of summer have not yet come ; the days are still

DAFFODILS AND TULIPS IN MUNSTEAD GLASSES.

PARROT AND RETROFLEXA. TULIPS IN AN ITALIAN
DRUG JAR.

fairly restful, and one is so glad to greet and handle these early blossoms. There are not as yet too many flowers. The abundance of June, with its many floral distractions, is not yet upon one. Moreover, the early flowers that come on slowly last long in water. The flowers of middle and late summer, pushing quickly into life, much sooner fade; they come and go in a hurry—one feels that the time spent in setting them up is somewhat wasted. But the steadfast Tulips will last for nearly a week, thus giving a better return for the time devoted to them.

The Darwin Tulips, in their many varieties of tall-stemmed one-coloured bloom, are among the most decorative of the round-petalled forms. Among the splashed and striped mixed Bybloemen, the discarded blooms from among which the more regularly-marked show flowers are chosen, there are examples of the highest decorative quality. It matters but little for room ornament that the "flames" or "feathers" should be symmetrical; it concerns us more that the flowers should be bold and handsome. They are beautiful in jars of blue and white china, or pewter, of rather upright form.

Among Tulips the most refined of form (not considering show standards) is the clear pale yellow *T. retroflexa;* with its sharp-pointed turned-back petals. This remarkable Tulip is one of the most graceful of its kind; its freedom of form, and one might almost say freedom of action, making it quite unlike any other. Parrot Tulips have something of the same habit as to wayward contortion of stem. This makes

them a little difficult to arrange, but, when cleverly
placed so that the weight of the heavy head is ade-
quately carried, and the flower poised in accordance
with the action of the stalk, the effect is excellent.
Silver-crown and Sulphur-crown have somewhat the
same form as *retroflexa*, but less accentuated. Among
the showiest colourings the tall scarlet *Gesneriana
major*, and, later, the sweet-scented *T. macrospeila*, are
capital room flowers; and where the colouring is
suitable, the tall and large Bleu Celeste is a grand
object. It is absurdly named, for no tulip is anything
like blue. It is a double Tulip of massive form of a
rather subdued and yet effective purple colour, and is
among the latest.

The third week of May is the week of Lily of the
Valley. It is intensely sweet in rooms, and needs no
description or extolling. It is best in glasses quite by
itself.

There is an early Rhododendron of rather small
habit called Cunningham's White, which is a treasured
kind for cutting. Its white is faintly tinged with lilac.
It is charming in a roomy bowl, either alone or with
white and purple Tulips.

The finest strain of the white and yellow Bunch
Primroses is not at its best till near the middle of
May. They are fine things in bowls of blue and white
china, but are thankful for a preparation of an hour or
two up to their necks in water; this quite doubles
their power of endurance.

There is a little-known shrub whose flowers in early
May are of the greatest value. It is *Laurustinus*

WHITE TULIPS IN A MUNSTEAD GLASS.

WHITE LILAC "MARIE LEGRAYE."

lucidus, less hardy than the one usually grown, but flowering well in sheltered places in our southern counties. The blooms are pure white, and much finer than those of the common kind; the leaves are larger and highly polished. Where this does well, Choisya will also flourish, and give its bunches of pretty bloom—so like orange-blossom—all through May.

Dielytra and Solomon's Seal will be in every garden where good cutting plants are grown, and Pansies in quantity. Pansies are not so often grown for indoor use as they deserve; perhaps because people do not think of the best way of using them. This is to cut, not the bloom only, but the whole shoot. When fair-sized sorts are grown, they can be cut nine inches long. They are delightful in wide bowls with the colours properly assorted, as white and yellow, white and blue, or white and purple together, and the rich and pale purples mixed; and the rich browns of the wallflower colours, either with or without the deeper yellows.

Then let anyone try a bowl of Woodruff and Forget-me-not, with a few pure white Pansies; and enjoy, not their pleasant fresh colouring only, but their faint perfumes, so evenly balanced and so kindly blending.

The last fortnight of May brings the Lilacs, now in many beautiful varieties, thanks to the unceasing labours of some of the best nurserymen of France. The whites are always beautiful alone, but white and lilac, especially those of the pinkish tinge, such as the one named Lucie Baltet, are charming together. One

of the best whites, and one of the easiest to grow is
Marie Legraye.

There is a pretty Himalayan bramble, the double
Rubus rosœfolius, not often cultivated, that yields
charming sprays for cutting in May. It is hardy in
the South of England, but except in the most favoured
districts does not flower out of doors. It is well worth
a place in the unheated greenhouse.

By the middle of May Laburnum and white Broom
are in flower ; they arrange charmingly together with
young oak foliage of a pale or yellowish green colour.

Stachys lanata, with its grey, plush-like leaves, one
of the most useful garden plants for informal edgings
where grey colouring is desired, is much improved by
the removal of the flowering shoots which are now
nearly a foot high. These shoots are of great use in
flower arrangements, well suiting anything of pink,
white or lilac colouring, or a combination of all
three.

There is a free-blooming white Stock called White
Cloud, which, although it is a single flower, is a
delightful thing in a room. It is pretty with these
shoots of Stachys, a few bits of London Pride, and
one or two China Roses. China Rose and Rosemary
are also sympathetic companions both indoors and
out.

In the middle of the month the herbaceous Peonies
will have been in bloom. In the garden they should
be planted in half shade, for they burn and soon go off
in the sun. A shady place also better suits their rich
colouring. We have them intergrouped with hardy

RUBUS ROSÆFOLIUS.

TREE PEONIES AND CLEMATIS MONTANA IN A LARGE GLASS TAZZA.

ferns, the Male Fern and the Lady Fern and *Funkia
Sieboldi.* They are fine in rooms set up in something
large, such as a Venetian copper wine-cooler, with the
same accompaniment. But, as in the case of orchids,
it is much better if the fern is a whole plant growing in
a pot.

The end of May brings the first of the Tree Peonies.
They cannot be cut with long stalks as in the case of
the herbaceous kinds, and therefore are best arranged
in something of large bowl form. I have a very large
and heavy old glass *tazza* that holds them well. They
are pretty with some early sprays of *Clematis montana.*

CHAPTER IV

JUNE

THE flowers of early June begin with the ever-welcome Guelder Rose, Tree Lupines, perennial Lupines, the sweet old White Pink, and, with these, the gorgeous Oriental Poppy. The Poppy indeed began in May but may well be classed among June flowers. One often hears it said that this grand Poppy will not live in water. This is by no means the case, though it is easy to see why it is so generally believed. Poppies and some other flowers, have a milky juice which has the property of drying quickly. If they are cut and not put in water immediately, this juice dries and seals up the cut end of the stalk so that it cannot draw up water. The stalk should be freshly cut and also slit up the moment before it is put in the water ; then the milky juice is washed away and the flowers live quite as long as any others of the time of year.

Guelder Rose is charming arranged with *Clematis montana*, and perhaps one or two of the rose-coloured herbaceous Peonies that will still be in bloom. These Peonies are in three colourings, deep crimson, rose-coloured, and a pale pink that fades to a dull white. Guelder Rose and all other hardwooded flowers should have their woody stems slit up, or a strip or two of

54

"The end of May brings the first of the Tree Peonies. They cannot be cut with long stalks as in the case of the herbaceous kinds, and are therefore best arranged in something of a large bowl form."

IRIS AND ARTICHOKE LEAVES; STOCK WHITE CLOUD
AND STACHYS IN MUNSTEAD GLASSES.

the bark should be torn up for two or three inches. They naturally take up water with more difficulty than flowers with more fleshy stalks, and are therefore helped by any treatment that presents a larger expanse of raw tissue to the water.

The flag-leaved Irises are grand cutting flowers. For large arrangements they should be cut as long as possible and set up with Artichoke leaves that have had a bath of complete immersion, with the cut end slit up, in a tank or water-barrow.

The pretty Brier Roses, white, pink and rosy crimson, are charming in bowls and deep dishes. The earliest to bloom, and by no means the least charming, is the wild Burnet Rose (*Rosa spinosissima*), that grows in many moorlands and rough places, generally not far from the sea. It is the parent of all the double Scotch Briers.

Rhododendrons, cut long and boldly arranged, are fine things in a room. In cutting them it is well to choose branches that grow nearly upright. Those that lean outwards are tempting from their more graceful form, but, when they are cut two to three feet long, their heads are so heavy that they are almost unmanageable, unless they are in something strong and heavy, such as a bronze jar, in which they can be tightly wedged. Clear whites and purples are beautiful together, also whites, true pinks, and the fine reds that incline to scarlet and blood-colour. There is an old Rhododendron, of tender white colouring with a blotch of scarlet spots, whose leaves are long and pointed, deep green and polished. Is is called Multi-

MEGASEA CORDIFOLIA MAJOR IN ITALIAN EARTHENWARE.

RHODODENDRONS IN A JAR OF GERMAN "GRES" STONEWARE.

maculatum. I am sorry to hear that in some nurseries it is being thrown out of cultivation, no doubt because the flowers have rather narrow petals, and therefore do not come up to the florists' standard. But it is one of the prettiest of all for cutting.

Of the Columbines, the most suitable for rooms are the long-spurred yellow ones derived from the Californian *Aquilegia chrysantha*. They are more graceful and spreading in habit than the *vulgaris* group, the best of which is a fine white of massive form.

The Ghent Azaleas are glorious flowers indoors, and though hard-wooded, last well in water. The whites and yellows are charming together ; indeed, so happily are they all coloured, that almost any may be put together without fear of discord. The best form of the white, called Viscocephala, is a flower of remarkable beauty. Fama is a brilliant rose-colour, Gloria Mundi a gorgeous deep orange, Nancy Waterer a large soft orange of charming quality. But all or any are desirable.

There is an Azalea that blooms towards the end of the month, of supreme beauty and charm. It is the Californian *A. occidentalis*. It is rarely seen in gardens, perhaps because it has the character of being a shy bloomer. The flowers are white or pinkish-white, the form is adorable, the perfume delicious. The leaves are graceful and have a polished surface, and are of more importance than those of the Ghent varieties. It is one of the flowers of the year that gives me the most complete enjoyment, and for cutting it is the best of all its beautiful kind.

AZALEA OCCIDENTALIS IN A VENETIAN GLASS.

ABUTILON VITIFOLIUM.

SINGLE PEONY, ABUTILON, OLEARIA GUNNI AND
POLYGONUM BALDSCHUANICUM IN A
MUNSTEAD GLASS.

ROSE AND KALMIA IN PEWTER; ROSE, KALMIA AND STACHYS IN EMBOSSED COPPER.

*ROSE MME. ALFRED CARRIÈRE, CUT WITH STEMS
3 to 4 FEET LONG.*

PEONY AND KALMIA.

The middle of June brings the Peonies of the albi-
flora group ; they are among the finest of the summer
flowers. They should be seen in flower and selected
for colour, for many of the varieties tend to magenta
and crimson-reds of that dangerous class of which the
word "amaranth" in catalogues is a timely danger-
signal.

Abutilon vitifolium, a Chilian shrub, is hardy in our
southern counties against warm walls. How valuable
a plant it is for cutting can hardly be known, for, even
in gardens where it would do well, it is rarely to be
seen. Like other tender shrubs, it should be well pro-
tected the first and second years after planting. The
larger flowers, of a very pleasant shade of soft, pale
lilac, are borne in loose clusters and last well in water.
It can be cut in large branches, and, with anything
white, such as *Clematis montana*, Peony, or tall Iris, it
makes a refined and charming room ornament of rather
bold character.

The Water Forget-me-not (*Myosotis palustris*) is so
familiar as a plant of water edges that we are apt to
forget how well it does in the general garden. Though
it prefers to be in damp ground, it is quite willing to
prosper in any place not actually arid, and is useful in
half-shady places. It is a charming carpeting plant to
Tea Roses of tender colourings, and suits them equally
well indoors. It does best with Malmaison or other
Roses of a pale, cool pink colour, and is pretty with
white Pinks and pale China Roses. In dry weather
China Roses have a deeper colour, but there may
generally be found some flowers of that tender,

shaded pink that we know as their usual and best colouring.

Every one knows what capital room flowers the Spanish Irises are. They should be largely grown in the garden for cutting, taking care that a good proportion of them are the clear whites and yellows.

The third week of June gives the Orange Lily in perfection. It is well grown and cheaply sold by the Dutch bulb merchants. It is a grand thing in halls or any rooms where its strong colour is right, and it tells magnificently against oak panelling. The end of the month gives us two first-rate garden flowers that harmonise beautifully both indoors and out. They are the lovely pale blue Delphinium Belladonna and the fine herbaceous Clematis, *C. recta* ; a plant of the highest merit and yet not often seen in gardens. The blue of the Delphinium is of the purest and rarest quality ; the flower of the Clematis is cream-white. They should be set up together with a few of the clear green leaves of *Funkia grandiflora*.

In the last days of June there will be Canterbury Bells. We grow them in three colours ; white, pink and pale lilac for preference. They are admirable as cut flowers ; no summer blooms last better in water. The cup-and-saucer variety is the best form ; the outer frill or flounce enriching the flower. Canterbury Bells can also be potted when just about to open, appearing to take no notice of what many people would consider a hazardous operation at so late a time of their life.

CANTERBURY BELLS IN AN INDIAN BRASS "LOTAH."

ROSE GLOIRE LYONNAISE IN SILVER BOWL.

CHAPTER V

JULY

THE first half of July brings the main bloom of Roses. All kinds of Roses, in their many ways, adapt themselves to good room treatment. There is a delightful freshness of sweet scent in a room newly decked with many Roses, although some that are really sweet do not give off their perfume freely. They are "fast flowers of their smell," as Bacon says. But the warmth of a room brings out as much of the perfume as can be given off.

It may be taken as a general rule that the splendid blooms of the Hybrid Perpetuals are best arranged in low bowls. What, indeed, is more delightful than a silver bowl, or one of blue and white china, full of fresh Roses! But to arrange a bowl comfortably there must be some contrivance for keeping the heavy-headed flowers from falling out. Several things have been invented; but I have a home-made contrivance that seems to me more practical than anything I can buy. It will be described at length in a later chapter.

The Tea and Hybrid Tea Roses can be cut much longer, and do well in vases of tall shape. The present abundance of pretty garden Roses can be used in many ways. Some heavy pot, bronze for preference,

with a narrow neck, set shoulder high on a tall chest
or cabinet with a thickly-bloomed long spray of a free-
growing Cluster Rose, is a beautiful thing in a room.
But it will probably want to be firmly wedged, or the
heavy head, unchecked, will go its own way, and that
way is generally with the clusters downward.

Sweet Williams are grand flowers in early July and
throughout the month. The strong, deep, velvety
reds of scarlet quality have a richness of colouring
that is hardly surpassed by any flower. There are
also the salmon pinks and pure light scarlets more
recently brought out by Messrs. Sutton ; all brilliant
and charming room flowers. But Sweet Williams,
fine though they are in the best colourings and mark-
ings, are not satisfactory in form by themselves. They
want something of more upright shape to counteract
the monotony of their flat heads. For this reason
they are best in mixed bouquets, with Roses, Canterbury Bells, Peach-leaved Bell-flower, Honey-suckle,
Pinks—any or all of these.

For large and tall arrangements we have the two
Sea Hollies [*Eryngium oliverianum* and *E. giganteum*] ;
white Foxgloves, Delphiniums and the tall white variety
of *Campanula lactiflora*. This fine Campanula, so
seldom grown, is five feet high ; it has large heads with
a pyramidal outline of pretty bell-flowers of a pale grey-
blue colour. Beautiful arrangements can be made of
it with a groundwork of the glistening silvery *Eryngium
giganteum* (the Silver Thistle) whose rigid stiffness
makes a helpful support, and another most useful
Campanula, the white variety of *C. latifolia* ; the whole

*WHITE ROSE, DELPHINIUM AND ERYNGIUM IN A
PEWTER TANKARD; SINGLE WHITE ROSE
IN A VENETIAN GLASS.*

Offering some suggestions about the use of wild flowers and foliage in the home, Gertrude Jekyll wrote: "June brings flowers in plenty... Now is the time of beautiful Grasses. Every roadside and field footpath is bordered with them; there are only too many to choose from. Try Scarlet Poppies and Ox-eye Daisies and Grasses together; choosing the Poppies in whole plants of moderate size and cutting them below ground so that you have the top of the root-stock. Remember that Poppies have a milky juice that dries quickly, so that it is well to make a fresh cut at home just before they are put in water."

made brilliant with some sprays of white Everlasting Pea, one of the best and most enduring of July flowers, or with the bright white Daisy flowers of Chrysanthemum maximum or of Achillea, The Pearl.

July has also some excellent cutting flowers of yellow colouring—nearly always decorative in rooms. Among the best of these are *Coreopsis lanceolata*, brilliant and long lasting, *Buphthalmum*, the yellow Spanish Broom, *Helenium pumilum*, *Anthemis tinctoria* in several shades of yellow, and Gaillardias. In choosing Gaillardias in a nursery, the proportion of the red ring in the centre of the flower should be noticed. There are many variations, but there is just one point where the width of the red ring gives just the best brightness to the flower. Where this red belt is unduly widened the flower becomes dull and heavy.

Among the best of cutting flowers, beautiful and long-lasting, are the Alströmerias, both the yellow and orange *A. aurea*, and in its better variety, *A. aurantiaca*, and the variously coloured *A. chilensis*. These vary in tinting, from pinkish white or flesh colour, through soft yellow, orange and charming shades of full and rosy pink, to red. All the colourings go well together. They have no effective foliage of their own, but look extremely well with a few bold leaves of Funkia Sieboldi.

The lovely white Madonna Lily is, alas, too strongly scented for a room. The early-flowering Gladioli, the white variety of *G. Colvillei* The Bride, the variously marked and tinted kinds of *G. ramosus*, and one or two others of this class, are excellent room flowers. The bulbs are cheap, and they should be grown in quantity for cutting.

Sweet Peas should be cut in whole sprays as well as in single blooms. The number of varieties is now so great that it is easy to choose from among them those that will make the best colour harmonies, such as lavender and white together, salmon and salmon red ; rose, white and pale pink.

WHITE EVERLASTING PEA.

*WHITE ROSE IN VENETIAN GLASS; FORGET-ME-NOT
IN LEEDS-WARE FLOWER POT.*

CINERARIA MARITIMA.

HYDRANGEA AND WHITE EVERLASTING PEA.

CHAPTER VI

AUGUST

CARNATIONS came into flower last month, but are in bloom throughout the greater part of August. Charming as they are by themselves, they are still better with some one other thing either of flower or foliage. The obvious Gypsophila has of late years been rather overdone, although that does not take away from its usefulness ; but there is one flower with its own foliage that I consider is a still better accompaniment. This is the wild Clematis (*C. Vitalba*), that is so beautiful in hedge and woodland on chalky soils, and is so well-named Traveller's Joy. It seems to me the very prettiest thing to arrange with Carnations, as well as with other flowers of its season. At every joint, in the axils of the leaves, which are disposed in pairs ; set nearly at right angles to the middle stem, rise the clusters of pretty ivory-coloured blossoms. For use with Carnations, the way is to cut the long garland of bloom into sections ; each section having one or more pairs of leaves and flowers. Many of the long flowering shoots grow hanging downwards ; in this case the stalks are inverted, the end which is really beyond the flower being put in water. But it makes no difference. Of course, with taller flowers like Gladiolus the shoots are used long, but then something stiff and shrubby is also needed to give support to the Clematis. In this way Gladiolus, Clematis and berried branches of the Water Elder make a capital combination. The Water Elder is a native shrub, but is one of the best of garden ornaments ; for, though the flowers are not so conspicuous as those of its better known variety, the Guelder Rose, it has the advantage of the handsome clusters of red berries all through August and September.

To return to *Gypsophila paniculata*, it plays an important part in some favourite mixtures of flowers of white, pink, lilac and purple colouring, arranged with grey foliage. There is a charming refinement about the association of flowers of these colours ; we call them our Pompadour mixture. For these the flowers of August give the best material. We ring the changes on China Rose, Globe Thistle, Achillea The Pearl, Sutton's Godetia Double Rose, Silver Thistle (*Eryngium*), *Lavatera trimestris*, the old pink form, not the so-called improved of deeper colouring ; Heliotrope, white Everlasting Pea, Sweet Peas, pale pink and lilac, pale pink Snapdragons, and foliage of *Cineraria maritima*, China Asters, soft lilac and white, and some of the small hybrid Clematises of faint lilac colouring ; and we blend and soften combinations of any of these with tender clouds of Gypsophila.

Then for decorations of more massive character there are pink Hydrangeas, their solidity lightened with long branches of white Everlasting Pea or of Traveller's Joy, or perhaps a spike of *Yucca filamentosa*.

CHINA ASTER (GIANT COMET, WHITE) WITH CLEMATIS
FLAMMULA AND MAGNOLIA FOLIAGE.

CHINA ASTERS GIANT COMET AND OSTRICH PLUME.

For arrangements of brilliant colouring in August there are Gladioli, Tiger Lilies, and the Phloxes of glowing colouring, such as Coquelicot ; with long branching sprays of *Stephanandra flexuosa*, with its pretty red leaves of sharp-cut outline.

Helianthus rigidus, the earliest and handsomest of the perennial Sunflowers, is one of the well-lasting summer flowers ; for a strong yellow of a rather different quality, nothing is more useful than a good form of *Coreopsis lanceolata*.

By now there will be *Lilium longiflorum* in flower in the open. Its own foliage would suffice, but the addition of a few leaves of *Funkia grandiflora*, with their fine, simple form and bright, fresh green colouring, makes an even better decoration.

August is the month of China Asters. There is now a good range of kinds that yield long-stemmed flowers of free outline, quite admirable for indoor use. The best are those called Comet and Ostrich Plume, and of these the most desirable are the whites and the so-called blues, both light and dark.

No garden plant has been more improved of late years than the Snapdragon. The taller varieties are excellent for cutting, and last longer in water than any other summer flower. There are now beautiful colourings of pink, rose and red, all of the best quality, besides clear white and yellow ; some of the more recent having a colour that approaches a brilliant orange-scarlet. They are best in mixed arrangements.

These mixed arrangements are by no means the

easiest to make. Of late years there has been a wholesome avoidance of the older practice of putting together a number of different kinds of flowers without much thought about their relative form or colour. Then we went to the other extreme, and held that arrangements of one kind of flower at a time was best, or of two kinds at most. This is quite right and safe for those who have not had their eyes trained so as to know all the resources and possibilities of good colour harmonies ; but it is not enough for the garden artist who will be able to put together a wider range of colour material, and yet keep within safe limits. But it needs the keen and well-trained colour eye.

As an example, let there be taken white Snapdragons, pink China Roses, the tall Ageratum mexicanum, some pale lilac Pansies (their leaves must not show), some pure white Pansies, foliage of *Cineraria maritima*, a few sprays of Gypsophila and of one of the small hybrid Clematises of pale lilac colouring. Let these be put together, not tightly, but with a certain ease and freedom of outline ; the white Snapdragons standing well above the rest ; and it will be seen that there are no less than six different kinds of flowers agreeing well together, and none too many. These mixed arrangements are among some of the most beautiful, and a little practice in assorting one range of well-harmonising colours will show how to do it with others.

CHAPTER VII

SEPTEMBER is the month of Dahlias and of several other kinds of flowers that tend to large size and bold aspect. As a cut flower the worst feature of the Dahlia is its foliage ; it is heavy in colour, uninteresting in form, and dull in texture. In my own practice I avoid using it, preferring to set up the Dahlias, if on long stalks, with leafage that I think more interesting, and giving them a softening accompaniment of *Clematis Flammula*. The illustration (p. 89) shows white Dahlias and Clematis set up in a tall Munstead glass, with the bluish leaves of Seakale and the bright green leaves of *Magnolia conspicua*. This Magnolia, which flowers in March, is trained against a wall. Every year it throws out a quantity of front shoots that should be pruned back during the summer, both to keep the tree in shape and to induce fuller flowering close to the wall. But instead of removing these front shoots all at once, when they would only go to waste, we look to the Magnolia to furnish a good quantity of useful material to arrange with flowers throughout the summer.

Another way of using Dahlias is to arrange them with shorter stalks in some large, shallow vessel, sometimes grouping two vessels together ; the better to make one large effect. Flower vases are often too much spotted about rooms. Such a simple arrangement of two things grouped together allows of a freer use of material, and often has a much better effect as a room decoration.

The glasses shown are a large heavy glass tazza with a foot, a much-prized old family possession, and a glass milk-pan of about the same diameter or a little larger. The Dahlias are white and pale pink, with leaves of *Megasea cordifolia* and some branches of *Clematis Flammula*.

This charming Clematis, with its faint, sweet smell, forms a part of many of my August bouquets. It seems to suit all flowers, harmonising and softening their varied forms in its own pretty way. The illustration (p. 83) shows it with some of the late kinds of China Asters, that were formerly called Vicks's, but that are now catalogued as " Mammoth." They are fine things for cutting, having long stems. The large leaves are those of *Magnolia conspicua*.

The pretty yellow-bloomed *Clematis graveolens* is also in bloom, and is useful for giving a light effect. One has to invent ingenious ways of supporting these pretty things when it is desired that they should stand up clear from the bulk of the bouquet. A very slight support is all that is needed, but often it must be there. It can generally be found in the slightly branching tops of pea-sticks ; just a little fork-shaped piece will generally suffice, and, as pea-sticks are usually of Hazel,

WHITE AND PINK DAHLIAS WITH CLEMATIS FLAMMULA AND FOLIAGE OF
MEGASEA IN GLASS TAZZA AND PAN.

the neutral colour of the bark makes the support almost invisible.

There are now plenty of bold flowers for large arrangements. Hydrangeas go on throughout the autumn and nearly to November. Tiger Lilies are fine in rooms ; splendid against dark oak with red-leaved branches of the Claret Vine. Pink and white Crinums are beautiful with boldly-cut leaf-spikes of variegated Maize ; Cannas have their own grand foliage; the leaves of Chinese Peonies are in many shades of subdued red that can be used with scarlet and orange Dahlias, Gladioli, Scarlet Salvias and orange African Marigolds, and all through the month there will, in most seasons, be a good supply of scarlet-berried branches of the Water Elder.

Several of the perennial Sunflowers are now of use, and the capital double Rudbeckia Golden Glow, whose spikes are a great help in our bouquets of big yellow flowers, because of their free poise and good outline. We set them up with white Dahlias, *Polygonum compactum*, and the yellowing leafage of the hardy Vines of the Chasselas kind.

Tritomas, as cut flowers, have to be used with caution, for, though they are splendid objects in rooms, they have the defect of throwing down a kind of sticky honey-dew. There is no harm if they stand on a marble table or anything easily washed down, but they should not be on tables where there are covers of textile material, or where books or other things are lying about.

The bolder-growing Verbenas are excellent in rooms.

In September and October "we feel we must make the most of the flowers that remain. . . we do not hesitate to cut freely. . . for the summer picture is over, and we feel that at any moment a sharp pinch of frost may come and destroy what is left." Late roses with autumn foliage.

Such a one as the beautiful pink " Miss Willmott," if the earlier bloom has been cut over, will throw up strong stems of large flowers that are delightful with foliage of *Cineraria maritima* and a few spikes of the tall White Snapdragon.

Large bowls, such as old blue and white soup tureens, are also capital with the same good grey-white foliage and the wide, massive spikes of the great autumn Stonecrop, *Sedum spectabile*. *Sedum Telephium*, a native plant of woodland edges, has some garden varieties, with flowers of a deeper colour than the type. It is of much the same character as *Sedum spectabile*, but is a little taller. A bowl of it alone is dull and monotonous ; but it is surprising to see how fine a foil it makes to flowers of any scarlet or rich red colouring, such as the deep red Phlox Drummondi, the dark scarlet Snapdragons, and Dahlias of the colourings of Cochineal and Lady Ardilaun. A few sprays of the hardy Fuchsia *F. gracilis* are a charming addition to such a mixture.

Acanthus latifolius and *A. spinosus*, both leaves and flowers, are grand room ornaments, but the large leaves should have the stalks slit up and have an overhead bath for some time before they are used. Another plant of large size and beautiful effect is the fine old *Leycesteria formosa*. Although its tassels of purplish-white bloom have no colour-strength, yet the whole thing, flower and leaf and bright green stem, is so graceful and interesting, so full of fine drawing and artistic value, that three or four of its branches, carefully placed in something rather dark and heavy, such

WHITE DAHLIA AND CLEMATIS FLAMMULA WITH SEAKALE
AND MAGNOLIA LEAVES IN A TALL MUNSTEAD GLASS.

MICHAELMAS DAISIES AND HYDRANGEA IN MUNSTEAD
GLASSES, WITH FOLIAGE OF VINE AND
CINERARIA MARITIMA.

as an upright bronze jar, form a delightful object in a room.

Anemone japonica, both white and pink, is now ready for use ; a few late blooming pink Gladioli will go well with it. Ivy is in bloom, and is charming with China Roses, while the whole range of Hybrid Teas and Hybrid Chinas is giving an abundance of bloom for cutting.

The earlier of the Michaelmas Daisies are among the most useful of the September flowers. We set them up with the great White Daisy (*Pyrethrum uliginosum*), and white Dahlias, and the ever-helpful *Clematis Flammula*.

When October is here we feel that we must make the most of the flowers that remain. Unless the season is unusually mild, such as was the late autumn of 1906, we do not hesitate to cut freely in the big flower borders. For the summer picture is over, and we feel that at any moment a sharp pinch of frost may come and destroy what is left. So we have great bowls and basins of Heliotrope and late roses, and colossal arrangements of Hydrangeas, and we cut Snapdragons in sheaves, and the second blooms of Choisya in bushels, and side shoots of variegated Maize and Canna, and look out for belated Crinums and Belladonna Lilies that are flowering well in a snug place against the south side of a greenhouse.

The Belladonnas go into a pewter tankard with some Funkia leaves that still remain in a shady place, for most of the Funkia foliage has already turned yellow. Red foliage of many beautiful kinds can be found.

The kitchen garden was visited before the carrots were lifted, for here and there in the rows some leaves of a fine red may always be gathered. *Andromeda axillaris* is finely coloured ; the cut sprays last good for weeks. *Vaccinium pennsylvanicum* gives leaf sprays painted brilliant scarlet and blood-red. Old bushes of *Azalea pontica* can well spare a few branches, also splendidly red-tinted, and some Scarlet Oaks are kept in the reserve ground on purpose for the cutting value of their gorgeous October branches.

So the last of the good red Dahlias have a worthy setting of foliage almost as bright as themselves, and the latest of the perennial Sunflowers are given an equally harmonious setting by the use of bright Beech branches of gold and orange.

Among the other red shrub foliage of October one is tempted to use that of *Rhus cotinus*, the Venetian Sumach. But all the Rhus are poisonous things to handle ; at the time when it is at its best, there is other bright-coloured leafage in plenty, so I am content to look at it only—not to touch it.

The varieties of *Megasea cordifolia* have usually in late autumn some finely-coloured red-bronze leaves, always good in bowls with short-stemmed red Dahlias.

The earlier hardy Chrysanthemums are some of our best October flowers. Those of red, orange, bronze and bronze-pink colourings arrange well with some of our red bush branches, and the whites and pale yellows with branches of Golden Privet and Japan Honey-

*AMARYLLIS BELLADONNA WITH FUNKIA LEAVES
IN A PEWTER TANKARD.*

HYDRANGEA AND CLEMATIS PANICULATA.

suckle, whose veined and gold-splashed leaves are now at their best. White and pink Chrysanthemums we put with foliage of *Cineraria maritima*, and white alone either with the dusky grey-green of Ilex or the splendid richness of Bay.

But the flower-glory of October, with its unending wealth of bloom for cutting, is in the later Michaelmas Daisies, of all shades of lilac and purple, white and mauve-pink.

When the great White Daisy (*Pyrethrum uliginosum*) and the large-bloomed Aster Amellus are over (they are both September flowers, though they just last into October), there are still the best of the Novi-Belgi varieties and the Novæ-Angliæ, and those of the *cordifolius* section, as well as many others.

But as one feels the want of the beautiful *Amellus*, so distinct because of its large size, it is best to set up the late Asters with other flowers. The late blooms of Hydrangea do well, of palest pink and almost white colouring ; for late blooms, especially those partly hidden in the leafy parts of the bushes, are nearly white, and with them we arrange the low-toned pink of *Sedum spectabile* and another of those valuable small-bloomed Clematises (*C. paniculata*). This charming flower does for October all that *C. Flammula* does for September. It closely resembles *C. Flammula*, but is a little stronger of build both in leaf and flower.

From September onwards there are Czar and other Violets. The Czar are slightly hardier than the newer and larger varieties, such as Princess of Wales, but all are thankful for a little shelter from frost.

Among flowers of comparatively recent introduction, the varieties of *Cosmos bipinnatus* give some valuable late bloom. They are annuals, allied to Dahlias. The whites are the best ; the type colour being an indefinite lilac-pink of poor quality.

COSMOS BIPINNATUS.

CLEMATIS PANICULATA.

CHAPTER VIII

ROOM AND CONSERVATORY DECORATION

ANYONE who is accustomed to arrange flowers in certain rooms year after year must have observed how, after a time, the room " finds itself." How, first of all, there are certain places where flowers always look well, so that one always puts a vase of flowers there ; and how one gets into the way of putting other vases into other special places. Some day one thinks, perhaps, the putting of the same glass or bowl in the same place is only a habit or a piece of mental indolence. The thing is taken away—put somewhere else. It does not do so well in the new place and the old place calls out for it. It looks empty—unfurnished. One moves about the room, studying it from every point. Yes, it must go back to the old place. Then conscience is at rest. The thing has "found itself."

Then one finds out that certain rooms demand certain colours, and that different aspects must be differently treated. By degrees one gets to know the wants of every room, so that in the end the raid round the garden in search of flowers is governed by certain limitations, and the quest is thereby simplified.

As to colour one can only suggest very broadly that a room whose colouring is blue will be thankful for

white and pale yellow flowers with bright green leaves :
but if the walls are pale blue it will also be well
suited with very tender pink and grey foliage. A
green-walled room will also be well-dressed in the
very tenderest pink, but will admit flowers of almost
any colour except strong scarlet and crimson. A buff
or yellow room will take strong reds ; a white room
all colours, but, of course, not all at one time.

Of late years there has been so broad and wholesome
a growth of good taste in all classes of decoration, that,
with perhaps one lingering exception, we are no longer
under the tyranny of any generally-prevailing fashion
as to what we are to put as flower-decoration in our
rooms. We have shaken off our fetters ; we can de-
termine for ourselves and decide what is beautiful and
desirable, and think with only repulsion of being bound
by any prevailing fashion.

Such is our feeling now about the once prevalent
sheaf of Bulrushes in a tall trumpet glass in the corner
of the drawing-room. When it was in vogue the
fashions did not change so rapidly as they do now.
The young people of the present day cannot even
remember it. But it raged for from ten to fifteen
years somewhere about the eighteen-sixties and into
the seventies, gradually filtering down through the
classes, as these fashions always do.

It was followed by the reign of the Pampas Grass.
Now plumes of Pampas Grass, picked and prepared
at the right moment and beautifully feathered are un-
doubtedly handsome things and are capable of being
used in clean country places with great effect. But

some years ago fashion decreed that they must be in every London drawing-room. The revulsion was a long time coming, but it came at last, and then it was realised that after a winter in a London room the poor plumes had first lost their freshness of ivory white and had then become loaded with that well-known, evil-smelling greasy grime that their form and texture seemed specially adapted for collecting and retaining. Yet I have seen noble rooms in great country houses where groups of Pampas plumes, on stems eight feet high, carefully placed in tall Nankin jars, were a perfectly harmonious addition to the room decoration, and where, on a marble console, between two of such tall jars was one of wider shape, filled with the silvery pods of Honesty, cut in whole plants three feet high, with great handfuls of the red-berried pods of *Iris fœtidissima* and the scarlet Chinese Lanterns of the large Physalis.

All these dried products of our gardens are welcome ornaments to our rooms in the early winter, though there comes a day somewhere towards the end of February when the evenings are getting longer and the days are full of light, when we find our Iris berries and Chinese Lanterns shrivelled and discoloured, and, thinking of the spring flowers that are soon to come, we burn the whole thing up and are glad to be rid of it.

Following close upon the Pampas Grass as a fashion came the Palm in a pot; it pervaded nearly every sitting-room and remains to this day. I do not venture to say that Palms should not be used in rooms, though for my own part I like rooms best without them, only making an exception in the case of Palms that are quite small, so that they have about the same decorative value as a well-grown Fern. How often does one see in London, in quite a small room, quite a large Palm, with perhaps three leaves on long, naked stems ; a thing utterly absurd in proportion. My own feeling is that Palms are admirable in conservatories and other places, not living-rooms, where there is ample space to group plants of large foliage. Aspidistras, on the other hand, do not outgrow their right size in relation to ordinary rooms, and therefore always look well. Moreover they are the most long-suffering of plants ; enduring year after year in heated rooms, though they are always thankful for having their leaves sponged and for being put out on the balcony in rainy weather on any but wintry days.

But the poor Palm. How one pities those that are hacked about all through the London season ; that pass their nights in crowded, over-heated, unventilated rooms, and their days in travelling from one town mansion to another on the tail-board of the decorator's van. Still more do I pity, and think grievously misplaced, the unhappy little Palms that grace the long saloon tables of passenger steamers, and that drag out their wretched lives in a perpetual state of quivering unrest from the vibration of the machinery.

It would be waste of time and page-space to enumerate all the plants that can be used in room-decoration, although it seemed desirable to name most of those that should be grown for cutting in the open garden. All gardeners know the usual routine plants ; the Cyclamens, Tulips and Hyacinths for early forcing, followed by the sweet Cytisus, Azaleas, and so on. It will be more useful to mention a few things not quite so commonly used, such as Solomon's Seal and *Diely-tra spectabilis*, potted in October : and to draw attention to the great beauty of some of the double-flowered Peaches and other near relatives of the *Prunus* and *Cerasus* families. Our best nursery firms keep a number of these pretty things specially prepared for forcing ; they should be consulted during the month of October. *Staphylea colchica* is another plant that forces well as does also the charming *Olearia stellulata*. Some of these plants, both for room and conservatory, will be found a pleasant change from such hackneyed things as *Spiræa japonica* and berried Solanum.

There should also be in every cool greenhouse, where a space can be made for it, a plant in the ground— not in a pot—of *Daphne indica*. It dislikes pot culture, as one may see by the sickly yellow-leaved appearance of so many plants that are trained in balloon-shape on a wire support. But planted out it thrives, and yields a good supply of its deliciously-scented bloom throughout the deadest of the winter months.

There is one of the Begonias—*B. metallica*—that is not nearly so much used in rooms as it should be. It can be grown small or large ; its natural habit is to grow upright and rather tall. But the sides, though not spreading, are sufficiently furnished, and its whole aspect, as well as every detail of leaf and flower, combine those qualities of grace and refinement that are so desirable in a room-plant. The common Polypody Fern is at its best in the early winter. Potted in wide pans it makes excellent indoor plants, though it takes a year to get the clumps well established ; but then it will go on for several years without a shift. *Funkia grandiflora* is also a most desirable foliage room-plant in spring.

It is a rare thing to see a conservatory well arranged and yet it is easy to do it if one or two simple rules are kept in mind. The most important thing is to have an abundance of good greenery. Here is the place for the Palms and for anything of the Orange, Lemon and Citron kind, and for Myrtles and Camellias, with what serves as undergrowth represented by Aspidistra, Funkia and Ferns. With the green thing, well disposed, a much smaller number of flowering plants will be required, perhaps not more than one-fifth of the number usually seen, and yet the whole effect will be very much better.

I have pointed this out not only to owners of gardens but to many good gardeners, and it is gratifying to see how well they carry out the idea. In well-stocked glasshouses there are many interesting plants that people like to have but that do not necessarily amalgamate well with others. Their place is in the plant-houses. What is wanted for the conservatory is a fair number of some few kinds of plants at a time ; enough of a kind to make good groups well framed in greenery but not to have brought into it everything that is in bloom in the plant-houses at the same time. Here, also, for anything like good effect, the plants must be carefully selected for colour. It is much better to have a restricted scheme of colour for any such time, say ten days or a fortnight, when certain plants are in bloom that will group well together, and then to look out another set of quite different colouring. Something of sweet scent is as charming in the conservatory as it is in a room. Many flowers are very sweet but do not give off their scent, but fortunately among plants of winter bloom there are quite a large proportion that are spontaneously fragrant. There is the hardy Winter-Sweet (*Chimonanthus fragrans*) whose little blooms, floated on a shallow dish of water, will scent a whole room. Violets, too, give off their sweetness generously—quite a few will make a room delicious ; so also will Freesias, Daphne and Lily of the Valley ; and quite a small plant of the Australian *Boronia megastigma* will fill a large room or conservatory with its excellent and powerful fragrance.

Sweet Geraniums planted out and grown as little trees, or what gardeners call pillars, are delightful in conservatories.

Glass-houses of other temperatures than that of the usual conservatory gain much by a well-planned system of arrangement. A house of a temperature that suits tropical ferns and a large number of orchids is seldom arranged to give such beautiful effects as might easily be secured. Here no side or low light is needed, so that the walls may be built of rough stone simulating natural rock, so stratified that Ferns will grow in the joints and nearly clothe the whole.

Hidden shelves and pockets among the Ferns would accommodate some beautiful orchids. The middle space could also be raised rock ; in fact there is no end to the ways in which, by the exercise of ingenuity and good taste, such a house could be made both interesting and beautiful. The dipping tank, for instance, instead of being a visible naked ugliness of galvanised iron, would show as a mysterious pool, rock and fern-edged, and none the less useful. The path would be slabs of flat stone with open joints where seedling Ferns would take root and flourish.

Conservatories of more formal treatment are often spoilt by a flooring of coloured tiles, where plain flag-stones would be much better ; they are still more commonly disfigured by fancy painting. This is often (and most disastrously) blue and white of a harsh and glaring quality. It is much better to leave out the blue and to slightly tone the white with a little black and raw umber, especially avoiding the cold blue-white so much approved by horticultural builders. As for the outsides of glasshouses their inevitable ugliness can be lessened by painting the woodwork a cool, rather deep stone-colour ; again using black and raw umber. In this way many a glasshouse that formerly obtruded itself unpleasantly has been rendered almost innocuous in the garden landscape.

"September is the month of Dahlias and several other kinds of flowers that tend to large size and bold aspect. . . As a cut flower the worst feature of the Dahlia is its foliage. . . In my own practice I avoid using it, preferring to set up the Dahlias with leafage that I think more interesting."

CHAPTER IX

FLOWER VASES AND HOLDERS FOR POT PLANTS

FOR want of a better generic name for the things in which we arrange flowers, the word vase must suffice, although it brings to mind visions of the many and various unbeautiful articles capable of holding water that are seen in the windows of china shops.

As a rule it is well to avoid things that have much pattern, the chief exception to this being jars of oriental blue and white porcelain, which are singularly becoming to many kinds of flowers.

Silver bowls, cups and beakers are always excellent, especially on dining-tables ; but they look best on well-polished dark mahogany, as in the days of our forefathers.

The cream-white ware made a hundred years ago by Wedgwood and others that is commonly known as Leeds, but is more properly called Queen's ware, is also one of the best of dinner-table ornaments. It was made in a considerable variety of shapes, both for dinner and dessert services ; but the ornamental pieces, especially those intended for holding flowers, are both numerous in design and beautifully adapted for the purpose. Many of them have fixed covers of per-

*A MIXED BOUQUET IN LEEDS WARE: ROSES, CANTERBURY
BELLS, WHITE GLADIOLUS, AND CLEMATIS*

forated strap work, an arrangement that gives the upper part of the piece an ornamental value when not used as a flower-holder, while the perforations make the flowers easy to arrange. Others have a movable lid of rising shape and fine invention, also perforated in accordance with the lines of the design. The Lavender holders of this ware are well-known and also the hedgehogs, with holes for growing crocuses. But articles of grotesque or *bizarre* form are rare in this beautiful ware, in whose design the strongest sentiment apparent is a conscientious and successful striving for the highest degree of grace and refinement. The time when it was made, the end of the eighteenth century, was fruitful of good design in England; that of table-plate, furniture and architectural detail of house fittings being alike remarkable for the same qualities of purity and refinement.

These qualities in this beautiful ware will inspire the arranger of the flowers, and will point to the use of those of light character or of some grace or charm that shall accord with its own sentiment. Roses of pale colouring and loose, free shape, small foam-like Clematises, such as *C. Flammula* and *C. paniculata*, and the wild Travellers' Joy; Sweet Peas and Carnations, Gypsophila, the feathery Thalictrums, the slender small Gladioli of the earlier summer, and the pretty little hybrid Clematises of various pinkish and purplish colouring; these and flowers of like quality will be found the most suitable.

Flowers are always excellent in bowls and tall jars of Oriental blue and white porcelain. Tulips and

A MIXED BOUQUET IN A LEEDS-WARE FLOWER VASE: ROSES, HONEYSUCKLE, SWEET PEAS AND GYPSOPHILA ELEGANS.

WHITE ROSE "GLOIRE LYONNAISE" IN LEEDS WARE.

ROSES AND PANSIES IN SMALL LEEDS-WARE BOWLS.

PEONIES, FUNKIA LEAVES AND A GROWING FERN IN A
VENETIAN COPPER WINE-COOLER.

Roses, Peonies, Lilies—all look delightful in this beautiful ware.

In many houses there are the remains of valuable old dinner services, reduced by breakages to a limited number of pieces that have found a home in glass-cupboards, some of them so near the floor that they can scarcely be seen ; often, too, they are put away in china-closets. Search should be made for these, for the salad-bowls, and especially the soup tureens, will generally be admirable for flowers, both cut and in pots.

In the same houses may probably be found some fine old cut-glass junket-bowls and some of the large old heavy glass finger-bowls ; excellent for violets, and all the more easily arranged if a glass tumbler is stood inside.

Those who have travelled and have been on the look-out for room ornaments may have brought home various embossed pieces of brass and copper ware. In my earlier travelling days the round or oval embossed wine-coolers of Venice and other places of North Italy, excellent examples of simple hammered work in brass and copper, were to be bought for little more than the price of old metal. Now they have become rare, and genuine pieces fetch high prices. Quantities of imitations are made that may content the non-critical, and they have a certain effect in rooms. They are capital for pot-plants and for large flowers such as Peonies and Rhododendrons.

Then there is the glazed pottery of many lands, standing well by its own weight and holding plenty of water. It is not fitted for highly decorated rooms, where silver, porcelain and glass are in place ; but is admirable in modest homes, and especially in those that have the cottage character. In using pottery for cut flowers it should be remembered that there is generally some slight percolation of water. Therefore a piece of peasant pottery should never stand bare upon a table, whether of exposed wood or covered. A glazed tile placed under it makes it safe. In my own case, having a number of pewter dinner-plates, I always put one of these under any jar of pottery that I use for flowers. Hard glazed stoneware, such as Doulton's and the fine old *grès* that is still made on the Rhine, are perfectly waterproof. The *grès* is admirable with many kinds of flowers ; its quiet colouring of cool grey and blue suiting all colours except the purer blues. Flowers arranged in a large jar of this are shown on p. 59.

Pewter tankards are excellent for arranging flowers in. Their weight, when filled with water, gives a sense of comfort in placing heavy-headed flowers, such as Peonies, that might easily overbalance anything whose centre of gravity was not well assured. They appear in the illustrations on pp. 16, 64, 73 and 97.

A homely article of stoneware or rough porcelain with a coarse quality of glaze is too often neglected. This is the common ginger-jar, that can be bought of fair size, with its own capital contents, of any good grocer for something between three and four shillings. Its rounded form gives it the largest possible capacity for water, and I can strongly recommend a simple

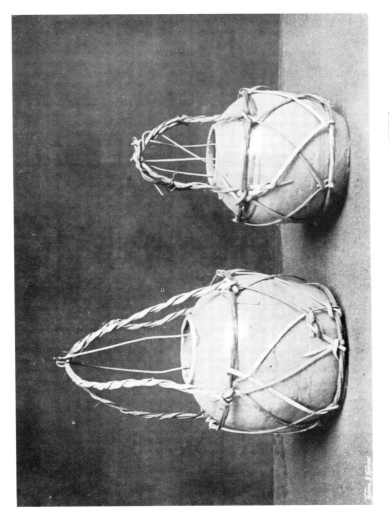

GINGER JARS PREPARED FOR HOLDING FLOWERS.

PREPARED GINGER JAR ARRANGED WITH FLOWERS.

contrivance by whose help flowers can be arranged in it with great facility either as bouquets of spreading or of upright form. I leave on the split cane lattice-work and bring the handles together above the opening. It is all the better if they cross each other. Then I bend some stiff galvanized iron wire, either one length or two, so that the bend comes where the handles meet or cross, and the two or four legs go down into the jar. The length is adjusted so that the wires strain the handles tight; the ends that are in the bottom of the jar being turned at a right angle for about an inch, after the manner of feet; this tends to prevent slipping. The wires and handles are secured at the top by being bound with fine wire.

Formerly it was difficult to get useful glasses for holding cut flowers. They were nearly always of a trumpet shape, widest at the lip and tapering down to a point just where it is most desirable to have a large quantity of water. I am speaking of something like fifteen to twenty years ago. It was so evident that flower-glasses of useful shapes and good capacity were wanted that I drew some shapes and had them made in a non-expensive quality of glass. This was undertaken at my request by Messrs. James Green and Nephew, of 107, Queen Victoria Street, St. Paul's. London. They are known as Munstead flower-glasses, they are cheap and strong, they hold plenty of water, and are in a number of useful sizes. A pattern sheet may be had of the makers. They appear in several of the illustrations throughout this book, on pp. 21, 26, 43, 47, 61, 89 and 94.

It will be found convenient in some cases to stand one of these glasses inside another.

Venetian glasses in some of the simpler forms are admirable for many of the smaller, lighter flowers.

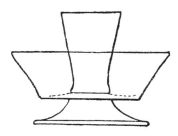

MUNSTEAD GLASSES

The beaker shape as shown, made in various sizes, is one of the most useful. I have some, in a very pale greenish glass with slight gilding, that are among my favourite flower-glasses. Other glasses that I hold in high esteem for holding flowers are some old engraved ones, with and without a foot, of Dutch and other make, but they are almost too precious for common use.

There are now a number of different contrivances sold to enable flowers to be more easily placed in

bowl-shaped or other vessels. They are so freely
advertised that I need hardly name them. I have
long used an arrangement of garden pots placed con-
centrically, one within another, for placing Roses in

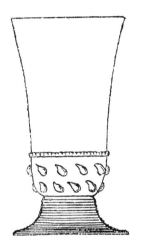

BEAKER OF VENETIAN GLASS

china bowls. The height of the smaller ones inside is
adjusted by a few crocks, or, better still, pieces of
coke. A little thin Portland cement joins the whole
thing together.

It is also convenient to have some inside scaffold-
ings of galvanized wire-netting made of half-inch or
three-quarter inch mesh, according to the size of the
receptacle. The netting should be in two tiers, the
lower tier raised above the bottom, and the two tiers
kept in shape and place by stout wire legs soldered on.
Any handy village blacksmith could make them, or

any town ironmonger would have them made to the size required. These are really the cleanest and most practical kind of supports. The upper tier should rise a little to the centre, like an inverted saucer.

In cases where it is not convenient to use such a contrivance, a few stiff twigs, as of Box or Holly, or bits of spray out of an old birch-broom, are a help in keeping the stalks in their places. There is also the way of having strips of sheet-lead about an inch wide, folded together like an old-fashioned ruche or frilling ; these, when stood on edge in the bottom of the bowl, present a series of loops that catch the ends of the stalks conveniently. But with neither of these methods does one get the comfort of accurate placing that can be had with the two-tier framework of wire-netting.

There are some English words which have no equivalent in French, but then there are a great many more French words—quite every-day and much-needed words—for which we have no English. One of these is *jardinière*. Even in French it does not quite rightly express its meaning, because the obvious meaning of *jardinière* is female gardener, whereas what we understand by it, and what we mean when we say *jardinière*, is a receptacle for holding pot-plants. " Receptacle " is quite a good word but has a certain stiffness. One writes " receptacle," but one scarcely says it. " Pot-holder " is uncouth—loutish. " Receiver " sounds like a part of a lamp. " Holder " is perhaps a little less rude than " pot-holder," and yet has some displeasing, though, perhaps, intangible taint.

"The early hardy Chrysanthemums are some of our best October flowers. Those of red, orange, bronze and bronze-pink colourings arrange well with some of our red bush branches, and the whites and pale yellows with branches of Golden Privet and Japan Honeysuckle. . . and other bright-coloured leafage."

HALF-DOUBLE WHITE ROSE IN AN OLD CUT-GLASS JUG.

What is one to do ? The thing is in every English sitting-room, and a general name for all the different articles into which we drop pot-plants is certainly wanted. For flimsier things that veil the homely garden-pot we have also no word, whereas the French have *cache-pot*. But this sounds like a soldier's rifle, and is still more undesirable for acclimatisation.

I therefore beg leave to say " holder" until some better word may come, rejecting *jardinière* as both exotic and cumbersome. It need scarcely be said that on the choice of the holder a good deal of the success of the decoration will depend, also that this choice must, in great measure, be governed by the calibre of the room, its style and its furnishing. It is true that a considerable variety of articles may be used in one room without offence, but this must be regulated by the individual knowledge and good taste of the owner. But the room will be all the better if any holders of large size and important aspect have at least a general affinity of design and style. This is especially the case with such things as are wanted for the accommodation of four or five pots of plants grouped together. For rooms of classical feeling there is no reason why they should not be made of panelled wood of well-proportioned rectangular form, with a properly moulded plinth and cornice, or with any enrichment that would be in character with the decoration of the room. They should be painted a low-toned white ; a treatment that would sufficiently show their own form and would be becoming to the plants whether of flower or foliage. They would, of course, be fitted

with suitable liners and some means of drawing off
waste water.

The French are particularly careful and successful
in setting up groups of pot plants. Some of their
groups are so beautiful in line and poise and balance

that they seem to be done with the same kind of
mastery of these essential qualities as that which
inspires the best flower-decorators of Japan. They will
put together one or two Crotons or Caladiniums with
Ferns, the whole surmounted by the feathery sprays
of a beautifully grown young Cocos Palm. The kinds

of foliage are sufficiently diversified to show off the several forms of beautiful plant-life in the best kind of contrast—the kind that is in fact a perfect harmony.

Among the best of holders are the old Venetian copper wine-coolers already mentioned ; but except those of large size, which are rare, they do not often hold more than two pots. Italian terra-cotta garden pots are now imported, and many of excellent design in the same class of ware are being made at Mrs. G. F. Watts's potteries at Compton, near Guildford. But of both these the rough surface of the baked clay is not generally suitable for rooms, though admirable in the outer air, in garden pavilions, porches, loggias and half-open entrances. There is, however, no reason why this terra-cotta should not be made suitable for indoor use by being treated as the Italian gilder does his roughly hand-carved picture-frames in preparation for gilding. They receive a number of coats of size and whitening, each coat being rubbed down when dry and hard. The carvings have the same successive coatings, but instead of being merely rubbed, they are modelled with steel tools into greater refinement and finish of form. The work is then clear-sized, and is ready for any final coating of paint, gilding, or whatever may be desired.

There is no need to mention the great quantity of coloured pots that may now be had in china and furniture shops. The best of them are always those of Chinese and Japanese porcelain. The ordinary so-called " art pot " has its uses in modest homes, but they are so obvious that there is no need to write about them, though it is well to advise avoidance of those of brilliant colouring such as the ones coloured orange and bright blue that are so apt to catch the eye obtrusively. There are also large bowl-shaped holders of white and coloured glazed ware standing on columns or plinths of the same, that are useful in many rooms. As in many cases their colouring is subdued, it does not call undue attention to itself.

Admirable beyond words, both for cut flowers and pot-plants, are the splendid bronzes of Japan, their quiet colouring enhancing that of every flower and leaf, and their strength and weight allowing the use of wide-spreading flowering branches that can be firmly fixed in place with wooden contrivances.

There are tub-shaped receptacles well made of hard wood with brass hoops, that are well enough in some rooms, and there have been attempts to suit wicker-work painted or gilt to drawing-room use, but never, I think, with much success.

Now that plants are so much used in rooms it seems strange that the want of really well-designed and other-wise suitable articles for containing them, such as undoubtedly exists, should be so inadequately supplied. Quantities of things are in the market, but with few exceptions, the quality of the design is not such as to make them acceptable in the best class of room.

CHAPTER X

DINNER-TABLES

ABOUT the decoration of the dinner-table it is only possible to give general advice, for as much depends on the taste of the operator as on the kind of material and receptacles that are at hand.

In large places the table decoration is usually one of the duties of the gardener, whether the table is arranged with pot plants or with cut flowers and foliage. This is naturally the convenient way, because the gardener knows what there is that can be used, and what fruit will be upon the table. Many clever gardeners acquire great skill and develop refined taste in their table decorations; and it is pleasant to see, in places where fine old plate and china are in abundance, how charmingly the gardener will adapt his schemes of form and colour, and yet vary the arrangement day after day.

As in so many matters that concern social life, the treatment of the dinner-table has always been subject to moods and vagaries of fashion. For a year or two one way of doing a table is "the thing," when something else comes in; what was right two years ago is hopelessly out of fashion, and some new crank reigns.

So it was that when we began to think of decorating our dinner-table with flowers—the time is well within my recollection—we passed successively under the tyranny of the three-tier glass tazza, the pools of looking-glass, the fountains, the blocks of ice; the elaborate patterns of leaves and flowers on the table-cloth, and the centres of bright-coloured damasks and brocades. We have been of late somewhat under the dominion of the shallow pool of water, and are now hesitating between the desirability of inventing something new and the better alternative of being guided by more rational motives.

With all these past and passing fashions, *as fashions,* I have nothing whatever to do. Good decorations, in good hands, have been done with all of them; and with every one of them good things may be done to this day if done just rightly. But surely it is better to keep the mind quite free, and to do the best one can with what one has at hand, whether the particular form of decoration happens to be in fashion or not. After all, the best components and accessories of table decoration can never be out of fashion. Silver, glass and china of fine design do not stale in one's estimation. A china bowl of lovely Roses is for all time an acceptable thing on a table.

Some of the ways of decorating tables that have reigned for a time as fashions have excellent features that ought to be enduring. The laying in the middle of the table of some exquisite piece of silken fabric, whether of coloured damask of fine design or brocade of colours with gold or silver, with one or more bowls of plants or flowers, and an outer punctuation of harmonising flowers in cups or smaller bowls of silver, china or glass, according to the material of the main bowls, should not be set aside because we have done it and enjoyed it for a certain number of years.

So also the laying of light wreaths of foliage and gems of brilliant flowers on the table-cloth might always remain as one of our obvious ways of decoration. When well done it is extremely effective, but like every other form of applied ornament, it should be done just rightly. It needs artistic feeling and a sense of *drawing*. It can scarcely be done from a recipe, but, as a suggestion, let us suppose a dinner-table decoration with silver candlesticks or candelabra of eighteenth-century design, and fruit and flowers in baskets and vases of Leeds ware. The flowers are of dainty pinks and whites, cluster Roses and the like ; and with them the white Jasmine. With this we lay upon the cloth a light tracery of the clear-cut Jasmine leaves, moving and crossing in circles and pointed ellipses so as to enclose the candlesticks and dishes respectively, the Jasmine-leaves being chosen of as pale or yellow a green as can be found.

For laying on the table we have to look out for leaves of clear-cut form, and for the most part pinnate, such as Rose and Jasmine, or more finely divided, as Pyrethrum or Cosmos—Cosmos " Klondyke " is a fine table leaf. If not pinnate the leaves must either be of distinct outline, as of the small Japanese Maples, Ivy or Virginia Creeper ; or, if they are what in botany is called entire, meaning that they are neither cut up at

the edge nor divided, they should be set neatly and
gracefully upon their stems, as in the case of *Andromeda
axillaris*, a twig of which is shown in the illustration
on page 138.

Where one of the ladies of the house is the decorator
she will find that one of the many interests of the
garden consists in the study of the kind of leaves and
little branches that will come in for the dinner table.
When plants grow in lissome sprays, it is all the better
instead of laying them on the cloth, to let them come
out of the flower vases and then to arrange them so as
to trail gracefully to form the lines of the design.   The
ever-useful *Medeola asparagoides*, called Smilax in shops,
and the two well-known trailing kinds of Asparagus
can so be used, also long streamers of Passion Flower
with its own lovely bloom ; best of all the splendid
scarlet *Passiflora racemosa* from the hot-house.
Besides these we have the two Wild Bryonies, one
with pretty little vine-shaped leaves and tendrils, the
other with heart-shaped leaves with a high polish ;
and Vine branches with pale yellow-green leaves, and
the wild Traveller's Joy, useful both in August bloom
and in October fruit, and three other Clematises, namely,
C. Flammula, C. graveolens, and *C. paniculata.*

Many another shrub or tree will give pretty leafage
for laying down ; some of the Andromedas, especially
A. axillaris, serving all through the winter for the fine
colour of its red-tinted leaves.   In late summer bowls
of Tea Roses arrange charmingly with the red-tinted
summer shoots of Oak, and well-chosen Oak sprays,
some of them also red-tinted, may be arranged upon

LEAF SPRAYS OF ROSE AND PASSION FLOWER.

*LEAF SPRAYS OF CLEMATIS, STEPHANANDRA, OAK, VINE
AND ANDROMEDA AXILLARIS.*

LEAF AND FRUIT SPRAY OF CLEMATIS VITALBA.

the table. But the right ones must be found. Perhaps no tree shows so great a diversity of foliage as the Oak. The edge of the leaf may be slightly or deeply indented ; it may lie flat or be strongly corrugated. In colour it may be of a heavy blackish or bluish green, or of a tender yellow-green or of some colour between that and a tint almost approaching scarlet ; while in length the individual leaf may be anything between one inch and seven. But a walk in woodland or by hedgerows where Oak is plentiful will offer a wide variety, and, for use with Tea Roses from July to October, we may find both the red-bronze of the summer shoots and also some of the yellow-green of small size with that well-waved edge that looks so refined and beautiful upon the white napery. Sometimes one may come upon small Ash leaves of tender yellow-green in hedgerows where stub-Ash was cut last winter and young stuff is sprouting thickly from near the root. Whether inside the garden or out among the fields and hedges, such prizes should be looked for.

The red-tinted leaves of several of the Rhus family (Sumach) are gorgeous in colour, but it should be borne in mind that they are all poisonous. It is better to see them on the bushes than to gather or carry them in the hand.

In the autumn months it seems natural to use decorations of warm and even gorgeous colouring. Not only does it accord with the sentiment of the season but good material is in quantity. From July outwards we have the charming sprays of *Stephanandra flexuosa*, that turn red as soon as the leaves are quite mature. It is a small shrub whose pretty sprays are produced in such quantity that it can always spare some for house use.

The coloured leaves of Virginia Creeper, and of its near relation, *Ampelopsis Veitchii* are of surpassing richness, under lamp or candle light, with Scarlet Dahlias and Salvias. With these it is well to have little bunches of the brilliant red fruit of the Water Elder, whose leaves are also red when the fruit is ripe.

When green leaves are used they should be of the brightest green that can be found. Anything approaching what is called emerald green is beautiful under artificial light. A satin, or other silk fabric of this colour, as a table-centre is extremely effective, although its colour may be alarming in daytime. But under lamp or candle-light the colour is acceptable to the eye because it is " glazed," as a painter would say, and acquires an added richness, from the warm-coloured light.

The flowers to avoid are those of blue and purple colourings. Pale blues lose all their purity, dark blues tell as black, and purples, unless they have a good deal of red in them, become colourless and heavy. Pale yellow is pretty with some combinations of yellow-green foliage, but tells as a warm white. Deep orange, and colours inclining to a bright mahogany tint, such as African or French Marigolds, Wallflowers, and the red-brown Pansies, are of splendid richness.

Pink, and light and dark rose-colours are always charming. The pink tulips of the earlier year, and

the pale and rosy Peonies of the more refined kinds of
middle summer, are noble table flowers. Sweet Peas
are charming on the dinner-table, especially in their
pink, rose, and red colourings. One need not even
fear at night some of the rose-colours that incline to
amaranth or magenta, such colours as in daylight we
should reject, for the yellow light of lamp or candle
neutralises the harshness, just as on a summer evening
out of doors the yellowing rays of the setting sun
improve the rank colour-quality of the Crimson
Rambler Rose. But Sweet Peas alone, on a large
table, want the addition of more solid flowers, such as
Roses.

All these questions of colour must be carefully con-
sidered and suitably adjusted, especially in rooms
lighted by electricity. The light given by different
systems varies in colour. In some it is nearly as cold
as daylight, but this is not often seen in good houses.

When pot-plants are used instead of, or in combination with, flowers, anything of red or of vivid green
foliage is effective. The red leaves of *Gesnera exoniensis*,
though only moderately red when seen in the hot-
house in daylight, are wonderfully rich in colour on
the dinner table. The colouring of the best of the Coleus
is fine at night, though generally too rank by day, but I
always think that its nettle-shaped leaves look unre-
fined upon the table. There are beautiful varieties of
marbled, spotted and otherwise coloured foliage
among the Codiæums (commonly called Crotons) and
the Caladiums. *Pandanus Veitchii* in a young state
is an excellent pot-plant for table use. Ferns are

pleasant under candle-light. The newer forms of Begonia, namely, Gloire de Lorraine and its varieties, and, Cyclamens are acceptable in the depth of winter, though the leaves of many Cyclamens, unless the plants are carefully chosen, are too dark and heavy.

Pot-plants in general have the disadvantage, when compared with cut flowers, of standing so high as to hide away some members of the company from their fellows. When all the guests can see each other the feeling of cheerful good-fellowship is unrestricted. Hence the advantage of flower arrangement in low bowls rather than high. The taller ornaments are in place when the tables are unusually large and long and the occasion is more ceremonious.

Many collections of plate comprise in some form the table centrepiece that we call an épergne. In the early middle of the seventeenth century, more than two hundred and fifty years ago, when some of the finest table plate was made both in France and England, the earliest forerunners of this article of silversmith's work were made. The designs remain ; probably many of the pieces. Their main features were a raised centre—some suggestion of an urn or casket supported by mythological figures, with that mixture of architectural detail and free arabesque that characterises the style known as *rococo*, that was in fashion in the reign of Louis XIV. The base of the piece is a long salver on scroll-work feet. The gadrooned and foliated edge of the salver moves in free lines, and the surface rises at various points in low, decorated plinths where baskets for fruit and flowers rise, and sugar castors and ornamental receptacles for small sweet things are placed, while branches for candles grow out of the raised centre. As a style, the ornament of this period may be quite indefensible, but such was the ability of the artists of the day, so just their feeling for grace and proportion, so free and yet refined the quality of their design, that it acquires a dignity which is quite undeniable.

Such table ornaments were made for great houses, with corresponding candelabra and detached dishes and baskets, throughout the succeeding century. But the *rococo* style never obtained any hold in England, where a quieter, more classical feeling inspired the designers of silver work. But the nineteenth century was yet young, when our national design in plate, as in much else, became debased ; and, later, when hand-work was replaced by machinery, and cheap, multiplied reproduction took the place of individual drawing and conscientious craftsmanship, the more ambitious the design the worse it appeared to be in taste. The greater number of the table centrepieces made during the middle of the reign of Queen Victoria are not now sources of pride to their owners. There was a favourite pattern of camels and palm-trees that was reproduced by the hundred—a notable example of the depths to which the silversmith's art could sink. At the same time there were pretentious articles of silver-gilt and gilt brass with hanging glass dishes, such as, in our more enlightened days, could not appear upon a good table.

So much for the Victorian épergne. The only thing that one wishes to hear of it is to know the meaning and origin of its name, and to be informed from what language it is derived. It has a French sound, but it appears to be entirely English. The French for épergne is, and always has been, *surtout* or *surtout de table*. The English for *surtout* is épergne!

The blue and purple flowers that cannot be used at night are in place on the luncheon table, and, especially at breakfast, it is cheering to see the lovely blue of Water Forget-me-not, with perhaps a few pale pink China Roses and white Pansies on long stalks, or a bowl of any freshly-gathered Roses with the morning dew still upon them.

Fruit and flowers are so nearly allied on our tables that I should like to remind my readers of a simple and desirable way of arranging fruit for lunch or home dinner. In small gardens there may not be fruit enough of any one or more kinds to fill separate dishes. But, if arranged all together, a few fruits of each kind make quite a good show. There is something essentially decorative about Melons and Grapes, but if there is no Melon, a small ornamental gourd will serve, or one of the cheap Spanish Melons that can be bought for sixpence in the fruit shops. In the case of a moderate household where fruit has to be bought, a modest expenditure will secure a handsome dish. Some important foliage, such as a branch of Vine or Fig or Hop greatly helps, and a flowing

FRUIT SIMPLY ARRANGED ON A PEWTER DISH, WITH VINE AND FIG FOLIAGE.

FRUIT ARRANGED ON A BRASS DISH WITH VINE FOLIAGE AND CLEMATIS FLOWERS.

spray of Autumn Clematis not only adds to the effect, but may help to bring the dish of fruit into harmonious relation with any bowls of flowers that may also be upon the table in which the same Clematis also appears.

The setting up of such dishes of fruit is one of the many decorative hints that I have learnt in Italy, where fruit so arranged goes by the name of a *Trionfo*. Indeed when Grapes, Melons and smaller fruits of bright colour and tempting scent are handsomely piled and wreathed with suitable foliage, the group adds to the table, if not a triumphant, at least an exhilarating, aspect. Any large dish, preferably of some metal— silver, brass or pewter, does for the base of the trophy.

The illustrations give an idea of simple ways of grouping fruit on large dishes. In England we lose by not having the handsome Melons of the Cantaloupe class, with their high colour, deep-cut segments and rugged netting.

Throughout the Levant, the home of Oranges, when they are to be brought to table, the fruit is picked with a short length of stalk and a leaf or two. When one is accustomed to see Oranges so decked with their own foliage, they look very bare with none, and the few Laurel leaves that we commonly put in the dish are but a sorry substitute. Little sprays of Portugal Laurel, with the smallest leaves that can be found, put among the fruits—not only under them—is an improvement on the usual plan, but better still are short leaf sprays of Japan Privet, for both in form and texture, they are much more like the leaves of the Orange. But it should be the ordinary kind, not the one known in nurseries as *robustum*. Little sprays of *Skimmia japonica oblata* are even better, as they are of a livelier green.

CHAPTER XI

WILD FLOWERS IN THE HOUSE

THERE are many people who live in towns within reach of country walks, or, who living in the country, have gardens not large enough to give flowers for cutting, or who are in such a position that they have no command of garden flowers. To these I offer some suggestions about the use of wild flowers and foliage.

Even in winter there is hardly a country district where woodland and hedgerow will not provide something worth bringing home. There are berried boughs of Ivy, and, for those who know where to look for them, fronds of Polypody and Hartstongue Ferns, and there are wild rose hips, and foliage of Bramble in its red-bronze and sometimes nearly scarlet colouring. Then there are sheets of brilliant mosses, and on hedge-banks little creeping sprays of small-leaved Ivy in much variety of colour ; some grey-green with white veins, some approaching scarlet where the soil is sandy and the sun has been upon them. These mosses and small Ivys alone are charming in flat dishes, and all the more enjoyable because wild flowers there are none and garden flowers are scarce, and the mind is not distracted from the quiet loveliness of the few small things that reward the winter quest.

A BOUQUET OF WILD FLOWERS: ELDER, COW-PARSNIP, DOG-ROSE, HONEYSUCKLE, SCABIOUS, DOCK, ETC.

Still our Bramble branches are not to be called small things, for we may have them as big as we please. Then, when arranged, we see what a beautiful growth is that of our common Blackberry—second only in form and freedom to the Vine, and not unlike it in its ways and aspect.

Then in February there are the little scarlet Fairy-cups, delicious things to put in a setting of fresh green Moss. One hardly knows how strong and cheering are these little jewels of winter scarlet, or how brilliant is the green of winter Moss, till one has put the two together. The Fairy-cups will be found in hedge-banks where there are trees; they grow on little pieces of decayed wood, generally under Elms.

By March there are the handsome leaves of Lords-and-Ladies, the wild Arum; they want a deep bath, as described in the chapter for March on p. 32. If wild Daffodils can be found, they go well together; but the Arum leaves are good alone, and there will still be some clusters of the heavy blackish-green Ivy berries. Soon after the middle of the month is the time to look for the wild sweet Violets, in the edges of copses or in low sunny hedge-banks; and in places where the small Periwinkle grows, its pretty flowers may now be found.

March is the real time for the beauty of Mistletoe. When it is gathered for Christmas the berries are not yet mature; in fact, they are not fully ripe till April. But a nice branch or two, put in water with some dark-berried Ivy, will show its curious and quite special beauty to much advantage; and if some shoots of catkined Palm-Willow are added, either when the catkins are in their early dress of grey velvet or their later garb of yellow anther, the bouquet becomes still more interesting.

April brings the ever-welcome Primroses, and on loamy soils Cowslips. In the Primrose woods will be wood Anemones. They appear to wither before one can bring them home, but a deep bath will revive them. In damp meadows and the edges of withy and alder beds there will be Marsh Marigolds, and in cool meadows, in a few districts, the purple Fritillaries. When the young green leaves come on the Larch, little branches should be picked and arranged in water indoors for their delicious sweetness.

In May there are Bluebells in the woods, and the early purple Orchis with its splendid red-purple colouring ; and young Oak leaves, golden-green, and for handsome foliage quite young plants of Burdock (*Arctium*) ; seedlings of last year. The whole plant should be cut underground and be given a deep bath of water for an hour or two before arranging. This is the Burdock of the roadsides, with broad leaves something like those of Rhubarb. The larger leaves on the older plants have their edges handsomely waved. In the younger plants, with leaves only from four to six inches across, the edges of the leaves are flatter. The other common roadside Dock (*Rumex*) is also a capital thing to treat in the same way for foliage. Both this and its near relation, the Sorrel of meadows, much like the common Dock but with narrower leaves, will also come into our wild bouquets a little later when they are in flower.

In some districts the Bird-cherry is a wild thing of woods and copses. There is the wild Cherry too, with bloom as pretty as that of garden Cherries; and in some woods of the home counties another woodland tree, the Snowy Mespilus (*Amelanchier*) has naturalised itself. Any of these are most desirable to arrange in rooms. Lowlier flowers that may now be found are the Cuckoo-flower of the meadows, and in woodland the lovely little Wood-Sorrel (*Oxalis*). This is best arranged in moss just as it grows.

In the end of May we have the beginning of a class of plants that will add greatly to the beauty of our bouquets throughout the summer. These are various species of the *Umbelliferæ*, common plants by all way-sides. The earliest is the upright Hedge Parsley. They are so numerous and, to the non-botanical observer, so puzzling that I will not attempt to distinguish them. The thing that is most helpful is to advise that they should not be overlooked. They are plants of the Parsley, Carrot and Cow-Parsnip character, flowering in umbels and common everywhere; following each other until the autumn, so that there is always a good supply.

June brings flowers in plenty. By the waterside the lovely Forget-me-not, the yellow Water Iris and the great yellow Loosestrife, and perhaps some bushes of the Water Elder, whose ball-flowered form is the Guelder Rose of our gardens. In meadows there will be Marsh Orchis and Ragged Robin; near the sea the

Horned Poppy, beautiful both of leaf and flower, and the Sea Campion ; on the edges of woodland Foxgloves and the still more useful French Willow (*Epilobium*). Here and there in loamy woodland we may find the surprisingly beautiful white Butterfly Orchis. On dry banks in light soil there will be Broom and Ox-eye Daisies ; on chalk the rosy-crimson Saintfoin, handsomest of native plants of the Vetch and Clover family. In hedges there will be Dog Roses and Elder in bloom —good to arrange together.

Now is the time of beautiful Grasses. Every roadside and field footpath is bordered with them ; there are only too many to choose from. Try Scarlet Poppies and Ox-eye Daisies and Grasses together ; choosing the Poppies in whole plants of moderate size and cutting them below ground so that you have the top of the root-stock. Remember that Poppies have a milky juice that dries quickly, so that it is well to make a fresh cut at home just before they are put in water.

In July, perhaps the best flowers are to be found by the waterside. The leaves and spreading bloom of the Great Water Plantain look like something from the tropics. A lucky search may find one or two blooms of the Flowering Rush (*Butomus*) or of Arrowhead.

In hedges and the more open parts of woodland there will be Honeysuckle ; in wood edges the tall Bell-flower (*Campanula Trachelium*) ; in woodsides and hedges also three beautiful plants of the pea and bean tribe—namely, the pink Rest-Harrow, the large yellow Meadow Vetchling, and the purple Tufted Vetch.

In cornfields there will be Cornflowers and Viper's

Bugloss ; in sandy places near the sea the Sea-Holly and the handsome Sea-Bindweed ; on chalk the pale blue-flowered Chicory, and in copses Daphne Laureola ; on heathland the pink Bell-heather (*Erica tetralix*), and perhaps in boggy places the sweet leaved Bog-Myrtle, and everywhere on dry banks the graceful Hare-bells.

Several kinds of Thistle that will now be in plenty are fine things for our wild bouquets.

In August again riversides and damp meadows will give plenty of handsome vegetation. The great Reedmace, that should be called Reedmace, not Bulrush, for the true Bulrush is the tall green rush with round section that is used for making chair-seats, and that has no value for room decoration.

Some years ago the use of so-called Bulrushes in rooms was overdone, but two or three at a time, showing up among other water vegetation, such as whole shoots of Bur-reed, and leaves of Water Plantain, with a few belated blooms of Cow-Parsnip, Tansy, Ragwort and Meadowsweet help to make a handsome bunch.

If one has access to salt marshes there will be abundance of the beautiful Sea-Lavender, and the curious *Aster Tripolium*, a flower that takes two forms. When it grows by the sides of tidal ditches where it is never submerged, it has the usual Michaelmas Daisy shape of a Daisy-flower, with yellow disk and lilac rays ; but when it is in places nearer the sea, where the whole plant is occasionally under water, the flower has the yellow disk only, and the general appearance

is so different that no one would take it for the same
plant. The same tidal ditches will also have the tall
Common Reed with its fine brown plumes. If there
are sandhills there will be the sand Lyme-grass
(*Elymus*), with its broad bluish foliage, and some
roadside just inland will be likely to give some good
spikes of Fennel, one of the most effective of wild
flowers for the house.

In heathery places there will now be plenty of the
common Heather (*Calluna*). Its soft grey-lilac colouring makes it more acceptable than the equally common
fine-leaved Heath (*Erica cineria*) and it is better in
form ; for if carefully chosen it may be picked in nice-
shaped pieces a foot or more long. It arranges
charmingly with both flowering and leafy spikes of the
grey-foliaged Wormwood, a few blooms of Scabious, the
white Hedge Bed-straw and Wood-Sage (*Teucrium*).

There will be berries by now on many trees and
bushes ; the black berries of Privet, the scarlet (with
a few black) of Mealy Guelder-Rose, both bushes of
the chalk ; and in wet places the scarlet berries of
another *Viburnum*, the Water Elder, besides the handsome fruit-clusters of Mountain Ash.

September brings these same berries in still greater
perfection ; the fruit of the Water Elder becomes
more transparent and gains greater refinement. The
Spindle-tree berries are opening their outer coats of
rosy pink and showing the orange seeds within. In
some seaside places, both on sand and on clay, the
Sea Buckthorn has its grey-leaved branches loaded
with deep orange berries. The Black Bryony of

hedge and woodland bears scarlet and green fruit, and the polished heart-shaped leaves have either taken a deeper tint of rich green or turned to a deep red-bronze, almost black.

Fennel, with its pretty yellow umbels and fine hair-like foliage is still in good bloom ; it is effective cut long, with yellowish foliage of Oak or Ash or Spanish Chestnut.

The illustration shows one of our September arrangements made of Bramble, Traveller's Joy in fruit, fronds of Male Fern, a berried trail of Black Bryony, Thistles, a seeding spike of French Willow (*Epilobium*), Yarrow, Mayweed from a stubble field and an out-of-season " puff " of Dandelion. October goes with September for its hedge fruits, and late flowers will be the same, but it has the addition of the beauty of yellowing and red-tinted foliage, of which Beech, lasting into November, is perhaps the most useful. Often in woodland, where undergrowth has been cut, shoots of green-foliaged Oak may be found right up to Christmas. Hawthorn berries hang long after the leaves are gone, giving the whole bushes a pleasant, ruddy look.

A BOUQUET OF WILD FLOWERS AND FOLIAGE: MAYWEED, THISTLE, YARROW, BRYONY, WORMWOOD, BRAMBLE, MALE FERN, ETC.

CHAPTER XII

THE RESERVE GARDEN

WHEN new gardens are planned, the reserve garden should not be forgotten. So many flowers are now wanted for house decoration that, unless some special provision is made for a suitable supply, the ornamental flower-borders would be sensibly depleted.

Such a garden for cutting is most conveniently laid out in rather long beds four feet wide, with paths two feet wide between. It serves not only for cut flowers but as a convenient reserve for all kinds of hardy plants. It is not for show, though it will always be interesting to visit, as any garden space must be when good flowers are grown in any quantity. It is perhaps best that the beds should have no edgings. They impede freedom of cultivation, and would be, here, a needless source of labour. Besides the hardy perennials mentioned in the chapters on the flowers for the months, there would also be the best of the annuals and biennials for cutting, such as Sweet Peas, Mignonette, Chrysanthemums, Lupins, Lavatera, Poppies, Sweet Williams, Wallflowers, Stocks and Asters ; also Gladioli and Lilies. It could be surrounded or cut off, if desired, from a portion of the kitchen garden or frame-yard by a hedge of flowering, fruiting and foliage shrubs, such as Guelder Rose, Water Elder, Snowberry, Spiræas, Lilacs, Golden Privet, Golden Enonymus, gold and silver Hollies, free growing Roses and Sweetbrier, all good for cutting. It is surprising what a quantity of useful cutting stuff a well-established hedge of this kind will yield ; moreover, the constant side and top pruning that it receives all the summer keeps it in shape and encourages the growth of useful twigs of bloom or colour-foliage.

Common sense points out that the sooner cut flowers are put in water the better, but there are some flowers and kinds of foliage that require special care or preparation. Everything hard wooded, such as Lilac, Spiræa, in fact, the flowers of shrubs in general, should have the stems slit up or the bark peeled up, leaving it on in ribbons, or the end of the stem should be crushed—anything to expose as large a surface as possible of woody fibre and inner and outer bark to the action of the water. Bamboos and reeds, or anything that has a hollow, jointed stem, should have a notch cut in the upper part of each joint that will be under water, so that the stem becomes filled.

Some plants have a milky juice that flows out of the cut stalk and quickly dries, sealing up the cut so that it cannot imbibe water. That is why many people think that the great Oriental Poppy will not live indoors. The way with these is to cut the end afresh and also to slit up the stem and to plunge it instantly in the water, when the milky juice is washed away, and the flower lives as well as any other.

Stephanotis has the same bad character, from the same reason. But if the stalks are freshly cut and the flower set rather deep in water in a shallow bowl, it lives quite well. For a long time I could not hit upon a good foliage to go with Stephanotis, for their own leaves cannot conveniently be cut, but the problem was happily solved by the use of short twigs of one of the broad-leaved Skimmias, either *oblata* or *Fore-manni*.

Some flowers and foliage whose stalks are of a rather fleshy nature, such as the wild Arum and Lent Helle-bore, should have the stalks slit up and have a preparatory bath right up to their necks either for a whole night or for some hours before they are set up. Flowers that come from a distance should have the stalks freshly cut, and have the same deep bath, of tepid water for preference. Anemones sent from the South of France recover perfectly with such treatment and last for a week in water. Hot-house flowers should never be put into very cold water.

Many people advise the mixture of drugs and chemi-cals in the water in which flowers are put. Mrs. London says a pinch of saltpetre, with the water changed daily, will keep flowers good a fortnight. Some advise ammonia, some vinegar. Charcoal un-doubtedly absorbs impurities and tends to keep the water fresh. But then fresh water is cheap—cheaper than charcoal—and a little attention in changing the water, especially when flowers are scarce and precious will be rewarded by their longer life without the addition of acids or alkalis. Then unless we know the chemical nature of the plant, such additions must surely be a source of danger. One would suppose that a seaside plant, for instance, that abounds in alkali might be killed by a bath of vinegar, or that a Sorrel or Oxalis that we knew to have acid juices would not flourish in an alkaline solution.

It is well to remember that all the *Cruciferæ*, such as Wallflowers, Stocks, Iberis, &c., soon make the water very offensive. Mignonette does the same. The water should be changed daily, and the stalks of the bunch washed before they are put back.

The most useful of the hardy perennials for cutting have been mentioned in Chapters I. to VII. Some annuals and biennials have also been named, but a more complete list of these will be found useful, and is here given :—

> *Ageratum mexicanum;* the tall kind.
> *Antirrhinum* (Snapdragons) ; tall kinds.
> *Argemone grandiflora.*
> *Bartonia aurea.*
> *Calendula* (Pot Marigold), Prince of Orange.
> *Calliopsis Drummondi.*
> *C. tinctoria.*
> *China Asters.*
> *Canterbury Bells.*
> *Carnation Marguerite.*
> *Centaurea* (Cornflower).
> *Chrysanthemum coronarium* and allied kinds.
> *Cosmos bipinnatus.*
> *Dianthus Heddewiggi.*
> *Didiscus cæruleus.*
> *Eschscholtzia.*

Foxglove white and giant yellow.
Gaillardia.
Godetia, Sutton's Double Rose.
Helianthus, Stella.
Helichrysum.
Jacobæa; white only.
Lavatera.
Lunaria (Honesty).
Lupinus Hartwegii.
L. subcarnosus.
L. mutabilis.
Mimulus, giant.
Nasturtium, trailing kinds.
Nigella, Sutton's Miss Jekyll.
Omphalodes linifolia.
Papaver bracteatum.
P. glaucum.
P. Shirley.
P. somniferum.
Petunia, large single white.
Mignonette, Miles's Spiral.
Salpiglossis.
Stocks, tall branching.
Scabicus.
Sweet Peas.
Marigold, French tall.
M. African orange.
M. „ palest sulphur.
Pansies.
Wallflowers, tall kinds.

It may not be out of place to draw attention to a useful form of basket for collecting and carrying cut flowers.

A few years ago, as it was impossible to find any kind of basket that was satisfactory, especially for flowers cut with long stems, I took some pains to design one. After a few trials, in which I was ably assisted by a local maker, a basket was made that I find entirely satisfactory. It is made in three sizes, viz., 20, 24 and 28 inches, and can be had either in

white or pale brown wicker, of the maker, F. Cobbett, 92A, High Street, Guildford. The design is registered. It is known as the Munstead basket.

INDEX

Abutilon vitifolium, 67
Acanthus, 92
Achillea, The Pearl, 75, 82
Ageratum, 86
Alströmeria, 75
Alyssum, 42
Amelanchier, 154
Ampelopsis Veitchii, 141
Andromeda axillaris, 96, 136
Anemone fulgens, 35; Anemone, 39, 41; *A. japonica,* 95; wild, 153
Annuals for cutting, 163, 164
Anthemis tinctoria, 75
April flowers, 39
Aquilegia, 60
Arabis, 42
Arbutus, 24
Artichoke leaves, 57
Arum, 13, 31, 32, 152
Ash, foliage of, 140, 158
Asparagus, 136
Aspidistra, 29
Aster Tripolium, 156
Aucuba, 9, 10
August flowers, 81
Azalea, 60; coloured foliage of, 96; forced, 107

Bamboos, 161
Basket, 164, 165
Bay, 24
Bed-straw, 157
Beech foliage, 96
Begonia metallica, 107
Belladonna Lillies, 95
Bell-flowers, 72
Berberis, 13, 14, 32, 39
Biennials for cutting, 163, 164
Bird-Cherry, 154
Bluebell, 153
Bog-Myrtle, 156
Boronia, 109
Bowls, china, 71
Bowls, silver, 71, 112; large, 92
Bramble, 150
Briers, Scotch, 57
Bronze jars, 57, 71, 132
Broom, white, 50; Spanish, 75
Bryony, black, 157
Bugloss, 156
Bulrushes, 104, 156
Burdock, 153
Bur-reed, 156

Caladium, 142
Campanula lactiflora, 72;
  C. latifolia, 72
Canna, 90, 95
Canterbury Bells, 68, 72
Carnations, 81, 114
Carrot leaves, 96; wild, 154
Chalk, wild plants of, 155
Chemicals, 163
Chicory, 156
Chimonanthus, 27, 109
China Aster, 82, 85, 88
China closets, 119
Chinese Lanterns, 105
Choisya, 49, 95
Christmas Rose, 14, 18
Chrysanthemum, hardy, 14, 96, 99
C. maximum, 75
Cineraria maritima, 18, 82, 86, 92, 99
Citron, 108
Clematis montana, 53, 54, 67
C. recta, 68
C. Vitalba, 81, 82
C. Flammula, 87, 88, 95, 114, 136
C. graveolens, 88, 136
C. paniculata, 99, 114, 136
Coleus, 142
Colour in room decoration, 103, 104, 141, 142, 145
Columbines, 10, 60
Compton potteries, 131
Conservatories, 108 and onward
Coreopsis lanceolata, 75, 85
Cornfield flowers, 155
Cosmos, 100
Cowslips, 153
Crinum, 90, 95

Crocus, 27, 28
Croton, 142
Cruciferæ, 37
Cytisus, 107
Cuckoo-flower, 154
Cut glass, 119

Daffodils, 32, 39, 41, 152
Dahlia, 87, 88, 90, 92, 95, 96, 141
Daphne indica, 107, 109
Delphinium, 68
Dentaria, 39
Dicentra, 39
Dielytra, 39, 49, 107
Dinner-tables, 133, and onward
Dock, 153
Doronicum, 39
Dried flowers and seed-pods, 105

Elaeagnus, 27
Electric light, 142
Épergne, 143
Eryngium, 72, 82
Euonymus, 10, 27

Fairy-cups, 152
Fashions, 133
February flowers, 27
Fennel, 158
Ferns, hardy, 53, 108, 150; tropical, 109
Ferns in pots, 29, 53
Fig, 145
Flagstones for paving, 111
Foliage on dinner-tables, 135, 136
Forced bulbs, 107

Forget-me-not, 41, 42, 49, 67, 154
Freesia, 20, 109
Fritillary, 153
Fruit, arrangements of, 145, 148
Fuchsia gracilis, 92
Funkia, 68, 85, 95

Gaillardia, 75
Geranium, sweet, 109
Gesnera, 142
Ginger-jar, 120, 123
Gladiolus, 75, 81, 82, 85, 90, 95, 114
Glasses, Munstead, 123; Dutch, 124; Venetian, 124
Glass-houses, 109
Glass *tazza*, 53, 88
Godetia, 82
Golden Privet, 96
Grapes, 145
Grasses, wild, 155
Grès stoneware, 120
Grouping pot-plants, 130
Guelder Rose, 54, 82
Gypsophila, 81, 82, 86, 114

Hard-wooded stalks, 54, 161
Hare-bells, 156
Heath, 157
Heath-plants, 157
Hedge flowers, 155
Hedge-Parsley, 154
Helenium pumilum, 75
Helianthus, 85
Heliotrope, 95
Helleborus altifolius, 18; *H. fœti-dus*, 20; Lent Hellebores, 32
Holders for pot-plants, 126 and onward

Honesty, 105
Honeysuckle, 72
Hop, 145
Hyacinth, 14, 20, 29
Hydrangea, 82, 90, 95, 99

Ilex, 24
Iris berries, 18, 105; *I. stylosa* 18; Iris, flag-leaved, 57, 67
Water, 154
Iris, Spanish, 68
Ivy, 95, 150, 152

Japan Honeysuckle, 96
Japan Privet, 41, 148
January flowers, 27
Jardinière, 126
Jasminum nudiflorum, 13, 23, 27
Jonquil, 41
July flowers, 71
June flowers, 54

Laburnum, 50
Larch, 153
Laurel, 13, 31
Laurustinus, 23, 35, 46
Lavatera, 82
Leeds ware, 112, 114
Lemon, 108
Leycesteria, 92
Lilac, 49
Lily of the Valley, 20, 46, 109
Lily, 85, 119; Orange, 68; Madonna, 75; Tiger, 90
London Pride, 50
Loosestrife, 154
Loquat, 27
Lords and Ladies, 152
Luncheon table, 145

Lupine, 54
Lyme-grass, 157

Magnolia, 27, 35, 37; leaves of,
    87, 88
Maize, variegated, 90, 95
March flowers, 31
Marigold, African, 90
Marsh Marigolds, 153
May flowers, 39
Medeola, 136
Megasea, 20, 88, 96
Melons, 145
Mertensia, 39
Michaelmas Daisies, 95, 99
Milky juice, flowers with, 54,
    161,
Mistletoe, 152
Mixed arrangements, 85
Moss, 150
Mountain Ash, 157
Munstead flower-basket, 164, 165
Munstead flower-glasses, 87, 123
Myosotis, 41, 42, 49, 67

Narcissus, 24
November flowers, 9

Oak, coloured foliage, 136, 140,
    156
October flowers, 87, 95
Ophiopogon spicatum, 20
Orange, 108
Oranges, with foliage, 148
Orchids, 29, 30; Orchid, wild,
    154
Oriental porcelain, 13, 105, 112,
    114, 131
Ornithogalum, 41
Ox-eye Daisies, 155

Paint for glass-houses, 111
Palms, 105, 106, 108
Pampas Grass, 104, 105
Pandanus, 142
Pansy, 49, 86
Parsley, 154
Passion-flower, 136
Pea, White Everlasting, 75, 82
Peach, double-flowered, 107
Peach prunings, 36
Peony, 50, 53, 54, 67, 90, 119,
    120
Pewter, 95, 120
Phlox, 85; P. Drummondi, 92
Physalis, 105
Pink, white, 54; Pink, 67
Polygonum, 90
Pompadour mixture, 82
Poppies, wild, 155
Poppy, 54
Poppy, Oriental, 161
Portugal Laurel, 41, 148
Pottery, 119, 120
Primrose, 42, 46, 153
Privet berries, 157
Privet, golden, 24
Prunus Pissardi, 36
Pteris tremula, 29
Pyrethrum uliginosum, 95
Pyrus japonica, 39

Ragged-robin, 154
Ragwort, 156
Red foliage, 96
Reed, 157
Reserve garden, 160
Rhodendron, 31, 46, 57, 119;
    colours of, 57
Rhus cotinus, 96, 140
Rock-work in fern-house, 95

Room decoration, 103
Rose, China, 50, 67, 82, 86, 95; Burnet, 57; Tea, 67, 136; Hybrid Tea, 95
Rosemary, 50
Roses, 71, 72, 114, 119
Rubus rosæfolius, 50
Rudbeckia, 90

Salad bowls, 119
Salt-marshes, 156
Salvia, 90
Salvia, scarlet, 141
Scabious, 157
Scarlet Oak, 96
Sea-Buckthorn, 157
Sea Holly, 72
Seakale leaves, 87
Sea-Lavender, 156
Sea-side wild plants, 154, 156, 157
Sedum spectabile, 92, 99; *S. Telephium,* 92
September flowers, 87; wild flowers, 158
Shrubberies, 9
Shrubs for forcing, 107
Silver bowls, 71, 112
Silver Thistle, 82
Skimmia, 149, 162
Snapdragon, 82, 85, 86, 92, 95
Snowy Mespilus, 154
Solomon's Seal, 10, 39, 49, 107
Sorrel, 153
Soup tureens, 119
Spanish Chestnut, 158
Spindle-tree, 157
Spiræa, 107
Spring garden, 39
Stachys, 50

Staphylea, 107
Star of Bethelem, 41
Stephanandra, 82, 140
Stephanotis, 162
Stocks, 37, 50
Stone-crop, 92
Stoneware, 120
Sunflowers, 90, 96
Sweet Pea, 76, 82, 114, 142
Sweet William, 72

Table-plate, 143
Tansy, 156
Tepid water bath, 162
Terra-cotta, 131; Italian do. 131; treatment for indoors, 131
Thalictrum, 114
Tiarella, 39
Traveller's Joy, 81, 114
Tritoma, 90
Tulips, 29, 41, 42, 114

Umbelliferae, 154
Uvularia, 39

Vaccinium pennsylvanicum, 96
Vases for pot-plants, 112
Venetian Sumach, 96
Venetian wine-cooler, 53, 119, 131
Verbena, 90
Vine, Claret, 90; Chasselas, 90, 145
Violets, 35, 99, 109, 119, 152
Virginia Creeper, 141

Wallflowers, 37
Waste products, utilising, 31
Water, Elder, 82, 90, 141, 154, 156

Water Plantain, 155
Waterside wild flowers, 154, 155,
    156
Wild flowers, 150
Willow Palm, 153
Winter-Sweet, 27, 109
Wire-netting contrivance, 125

Woodruff, 49
Wood-Sage, 157
Wood-Sorrel, 154
Wormwood, 157

Yucca, 82

Other books by Gertrude Jekyll published by the Antique Collectors' Club

Garden Ornament
12ins. × 8½ins./30cm × 22cm. 462 pages. 600 black and white illustrations. Garden design in relation to architecture — gates, steps, balustrades, garden houses, dovecotes, pergolas and many other topics are discussed and examples illustrated.

Gardens for Small Country Houses
by Gertrude Jekyll and Sir Lawrence Weaver
11ins. × 8½ins./28cm × 22cm. 260 pages, 387 black and white illustrations. This book is respected by generations of gardeners who continue to find in it inspiration in planning their own gardens, big or small, for the principles the authors expound are both fundamental and practical.

Colour Schemes for the Flower Garden

8½ ins. × 5½ ins./22cm × 14cm. 328 pages, 120 black and white illustrations, 32 in colour. Generally thought to be the author's best book. Her sense of colour, thoughts on 'painting' a garden and imaginative ideas on planting arrangements make this book a joy to read.

Wood and Garden

8½ ins. × 5½ ins./22cm × 14cm. 380 pages, 71 black and white illustrations, 32 in colour. The first book Jekyll wrote takes the reader through her gardening year month by month. Also included are her practical and critical thoughts on the herbaceous garden, woodland, large and small gardens, and other gardening topics.

Home and Garden

8½ ins. × 5½ ins./22cm × 14cm. 373 pages. 53 black and white illustrations, 16 in colour. In this book Gertrude Jekyll introduces us to her life both as gardener and craftswoman, and discusses in detail the building of her home — Munstead Wood designed by Edwin Lutyens.

Wall, Water and Woodland Gardens

8½ins. x 5½ins./22cm x 14cm. 480 pages, 205 black and white illustrations, 16 in colour. No one did more than Gertrude Jekyll to illustrate the possibilities of wall, water and woodland gardening. The richness of her imagination in relation to design and plantings only goes to underline what a supreme gardener she was.

Lilies for English Gardens

8½ins. x 5½ins./22cm x 14cm. 156 pages, 68 black and white illustrations, 8 in colour. Gertrude Jekyll's concise illustrated guide will encourage those keen to learn more about lilies, as well as excite those who, through these pages, 'discover' them for the first time.

Roses for English Gardens

8½ins. x 5½ins./22cm x 14cm. 392 pages, 190 black and white illustrations, 24 in colour. Though many new varieties have been introduced since Gertrude Jekyll wrote this book, her advice and ideas are timeless, while her writings on older varieties will stimulate keen rose growers to search out and cultivate good old plants which have long been forgotten.

The Antique Collectors' Club

The Antique Collectors' Club has 12,000 members and the monthly journal (not August), sent free to members, discusses in more depth than is normal for a collectors' magazine the type of antiques and art available to collectors. It is the only British antiques magazine which has consistently grown in circulation over the past decade.

The Antique Collectors' Club also publishes books on antique furniture, art reference, horology, gardening and architecture, together with various standard works connected with arts and antiques. It also publishes a series of practical books, invaluable to collectors, under the general heading of the Price Guide Series (price revision lists published annually).

New titles are being added to the list at the rate of about ten a year. Why not ask for an updated catalogue?

The Antique Collectors' Club
5 Church Street, Woodbridge, Suffolk, England
Telephone 03943 5501